WHO GETS IT
WHEN YOU GO?

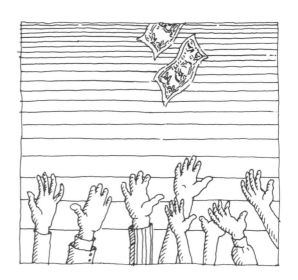

DAVID C. LARSEN

Random House
New York

WHO GETS IT WHEN YOU GO?

A Guide for Planning Your Will, Protecting Your Family's Financial Future, Minimizing Inheritance Taxes, and Avoiding Probate

Library of Congress Cataloging in Publication Data

Larsen, David C., 1944–
Who gets it when you go?
1. Wills—United States—Popular works.
2. Probate law and practice—United States—Popular works. 3. Estate planning—United States—Popular works. I. Title.
KF755.Z9L37   1981   346.96905′2   81–51035
ISBN 0-394-70658-7   AACR2

Manufactured in the United States of America

9 8 7 6 5 4 3 2

FIRST EDITION

Illustrations by Steve Reoutt

To Pam and Jennifer

Preface

The purpose of this book is to explain in uncomplicated language what can happen to your property when you die. It is written specifically for the layman, not the lawyer.

The book takes an overview of a subject that many know very little about, but one that affects each and every one of us. The laws on dying without a will, wills, trusts, probate, and death taxes are numerous and complex, and change frequently. To try to make some sense of the broad scope of estate planning, I've done two things to make the book understandable and simple. I have chosen not to discuss every rule, every regulation, or every conceivable situation that might arise. Many of the exceptions have been eliminated, so that what remains are the basic rules that will give you an idea of what you can do to protect your beneficiaries and property after your death.

I have eliminated technical terms and "legalese" in favor of plain English. For example, I use the word "executor" instead of other terms—such as executrix, administrator, administratrix, administrator (or administratrix) de son tort, administrator (or administratrix) de bonis non, and personal representative—that may be more technically accurate but mean essentially the same thing. Similarly, where a choice arises between a technically correct but unusual word and a less accurate but more commonly understood word, I have chosen the latter.

Three final points. First, and most obvious, don't take any action solely on the basis of what you read here, but see your attorney, tax accountant, or tax adviser first. This book is not a "how to" book, but is designed only to introduce you to a complex subject.

Second, probably 90 percent of the rules discussed in this book are the same across America. Obviously, different states do have different local customs, practices, and laws that may affect what is said here, but usually only in a minor way. For example, a guardian of a minor's property may be called a "guardian of the property" in one state and a "conservator" in another state, and one state may require a bond while another doesn't. Again, the purpose of the book is to give you an overview of how the laws generally work. Be sure to see a local expert to implement your own specific plan.

Third, in an effort to keep the book to a manageable length, many rules, definitions, and ideas are not repeated after their first mention. The book starts with the simplest rules and definitions and builds upon them. I suggest that in reading the book, you begin at the first chapter and read through the chapters consecutively, even though you think a particular chapter may not apply to you.

The easiest rules are those dealing with dying without a will, and that subject is discussed in chapter 1. In fact, 70 percent of the people in America die without a will, thinking that they are taking the "easy way out." Chapter 1 explains why they are wrong.

Contents

Preface   *vii*

1. If You Die Without a Will   3
2. Your Will   *18*
3. Probate   55
4. How to Avoid Probate   *78*
5. The Federal Estate Tax and How to Reduce It   99
6. The State Inheritance Tax   *129*
    Putting It All Together   *134*

Glossary   *137*

WHO GETS IT WHEN YOU GO?

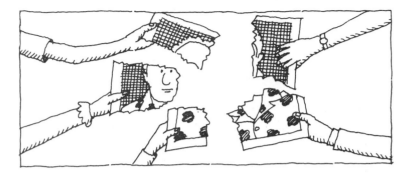

1

If You Die Without a Will

THERE ARE two ways you can die without a will. First, if you never wrote one. Second, if you wrote one but it's declared invalid by the probate court (see chapters 2 and 3). In either case, you are said to have died "intestate," that is, without a valid will.

If you die intestate, your state has special laws, called the "laws of intestacy," that control the disposition of your property. (By the way, "property" means not only your real estate but everything else you own too, from pots and pans to checking and savings accounts to stocks and bonds.) However, there are four types of property to which these laws do not apply. They are:

Life insurance and retirement plan proceeds. Whether you die with a will or without a will, life insurance proceeds are paid to the beneficiary you named in the policy. If you did not name a beneficiary in the policy or if all the named beneficiaries died before you did, then the proceeds are treated just like the rest of your property and are subject, if you die intestate, to your state's laws of intestacy. Retirement plan proceeds are treated in the same manner as life insurance proceeds: they are paid to your named beneficiaries or, if all of the beneficiaries are dead, to your estate.

Property owned jointly with one or more persons with a right of survivorship. As you know, most things can be owned by more than one person. Further, some of those items of property have their owners recorded at an institution. For example, a car, boat, bank account, stocks, bonds, home, and land all have their owners listed and recorded with some institution. If one such item is owned by more than one person, what happens to the property if one of the owners dies intestate? Who gets the dead person's share? Well, the answer is, "It depends." It depends on the way the "title," or ownership, to that property was held by the co-owners. Two or more persons can hold title to property in three different ways. Two of them avoid the intestacy laws.

Joint tenancy. Where two or more persons own property as "joint tenants with right of survivorship," when one owner dies, whether with or without a will, the deceased tenant's share goes automatically to the remaining joint tenant or is divided among the remaining joint tenants. The intestacy laws do not apply to the deceased's share.

Example: Mother, Father, and Daughter own title to their house as "joint tenants with right of survivorship." This title is recorded at the local county or state recording office. Daughter dies. Mother and Father now own the house as "joint tenants with right of survivorship": Daughter's share is not subject to the intestacy laws and is automatically merged into Mother's and Father's shares. When Father dies later, his share is not subject to the intestacy laws and Mother becomes the sole owner. But when Mother dies, because there are no more joint tenants with her, the entire property is disposed of by the intestacy laws if Mother died intestate, or by her will if she died with one.

Tenants by the entirety. This is a joint tenancy between a husband and a wife and no one else. When one spouse dies, whether with or without a will, the other automatically gets the entire property. The deceased spouse's share is not subject to the intestacy laws. It goes automatically to the surviving spouse. Later, however, when the surviving spouse dies, the entire property is disposed of by the intestacy laws if he or she died intestate, or by his or her will if there was one.

Tenants in common. If property isn't owned as "joint tenancy with right of survivorship" or "tenants by the entirety" and is owned by two or more persons, then it is held by those persons as "tenants in common." There is no other way it can be held. Under this form of ownership, when one owner dies, his or her share is *not* merged automatically into the shares of the other owners. If the deceased owner died intestate, his or her share would be subject to the intestacy laws; if he or she died with a will, the share would be subject to the will.

Example: John, Mary, and Peter own a piece of land. The deed describes them as "tenants in common." The deed states that John's share is 40 percent, Mary's is 50 percent, and Peter's is 10

percent. John dies without a will. His 40 percent interest goes not
to Mary and Peter but to his heirs. Mary and Peter now have new
co-owners.

Property held in a living trust. Property held in a trust you
set up while you are alive (a "living trust") is not subject to
the intestacy laws, and goes, at your death, to the persons
you name in the trust. The trust alone controls where the
trust property goes. See chapter 4 for more on trusts, which
have rightly been called "the most useful estate-planning tool
available."

**Your spouse's one half of the community property you and
your spouse own together.** At present only eight states in
America have the "community property" system. Those
states are California, Arizona, Washington, Idaho, Louisi-
ana, Nevada, New Mexico, and Texas. (If you live in another
state, this discussion won't apply to you.) In a state with such
a system your property is classified as either "community
property" or "separate property." Community property is
money, or property bought with money, earned by one
spouse or the other during marriage together. Separate property is money or property owned by you before your marriage, or gifted to you or inherited by you during your
marriage.

Example: John owns a car before his marriage to Sue. After their
marriage, John earns $100,000 in salary, and with it John and Sue
buy a house, furnishings, and stocks. During their marriage, Sam,
John's old friend, gives him a watch, and John inherits a condominium apartment from his mother. The car, watch, and apartment are
John's "separate property"; the house, furnishings, and stocks are
the "community property" of John and Sue.

When John dies, one half of the community property already belongs, under the law, to Sue. That one half is not affected by John's death. The other half of the community property, which was John's, and all of his separate property are subject to John's will or, if he didn't have one, to the intestacy laws.

John could have, if he wished, put his separate property and his one half of the community property into a joint tenancy with rights of survivorship or into a living trust. And, of course, he could have owned life insurance, and had a retirement plan. If he had done so, then, as you've already seen, none of that property would have been subject to the intestacy laws.

We can see this clearly with a diagram. Just divide your property into two boxes:

LSTC Property	Intestacy Property

Life insurance, Survivorship property (i.e., property held in joint tenancy with right of survivorship or in tenancy by the entirety), property held in a living Trust, and your spouse's one half of the Community property (LSTC) go in one box. All your other property goes into the other box and is the only property subject to the intestacy laws.

If you look at the right-hand box, you'll note that it contains two types of property: property in your name alone and your percentage interest as a tenant in common with other people. (In a community property state, your one half of the community property, and all your separate property, would go into the right-hand box unless you had put it into a joint tenancy or into a living trust, which is in the left-hand box.)

Let's take an example. Usually, married couples own their

homes as "tenants by the entirety" or as "joint tenants with rights of survivorship" (but check your deed to be sure). Their life insurance proceeds are payable to some named beneficiary. Thus, those two items won't be subject to the intestacy laws. But what about household furniture? Clothing? Personal effects and jewelry? The car in one name alone? The bank account in one name alone? The stocks and bonds in one name alone? All of these items, if held in one name alone or if held with others in a tenancy in common, are subject to the intestacy laws.

How do the intestacy laws distribute your intestacy property? Who gets what? (Remember, you have no say because you didn't write a valid will.) Let's look at the following examples. You'll see that who gets what depends on where the person is on your family tree. And remember the obvious: the intestacy laws vary from state to state, some states giving more of your intestacy property to a particular heir than another state would give him or her.

1. You (D) die. Your mother (M), father (F), spouse (SP), and children (C) survive you. (An X over the letter symbol indicates the deceased.)

$$F \!-\!\!\top\!\!- M$$

$$\text{\emph{D}} \!-\!\!\top\!\!- SP$$

$$C_1 \qquad C_2$$

What does SP get? This varies widely from state to state, but you can be virtually certain that SP will *not* get all your intestacy property. Different states would give SP one third or one half, or a certain flat dollar amount, or a certain flat dollar amount plus a percentage of the rest. Some states would give a widow more than a widower. Some community property states give SP all of D's community property; other community property states give it directly to the children and not to SP. Whatever amount of your intestacy property SP doesn't take goes to C_1 and C_2 equally. The equal split between C_1 and C_2 can be very unfair if you've paid C_1's way through school, while C_2 is just starting out, or needs special medical attention, or has other special needs.

2. Assume C_1 was already deceased at your death, and left two children (your grandchildren [GC]).

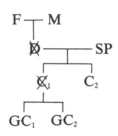

Here GC_1 and GC_2 split C_1's share.

3. If C_1 and C_2 both predeceased you, and C_2 left three grandchildren:

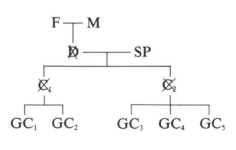

Then SP still gets his or her partial share, and the rest is usually split equally among all grandchildren, since all takers beneath you are on the same level. In some states, however, GC_1 and GC_2 would each take half of C_1's share, and GC_3 through GC_5 would each take one third of C_2's share.

4. Only if you leave no living "issue" (meaning children, grandchildren, great-grandchildren, etc.) will your parents possibly share.

$$F \overline{\top} M$$

Here SP takes his or her share, and M and F split the rest. If one of your parents is dead, the other takes the rest in most states.

5. In most states, if you leave no living issue and no living parents, your spouse will take all.

In this example, SP takes all of your property.

6. If you are not survived by your spouse (for example, if you are a widower or widow, or never married), then in most states all of your property goes first to your issue, as explained above, or if there are no living issue, all goes to your parents or parent. GC_1 and GC_2 take C_1's one half (getting one quarter each), and C_2 takes his one half. GC_3, GC_4, and GC_5 take nothing because C_2 is still alive. Similarly, the parents do not take because there are living issue.

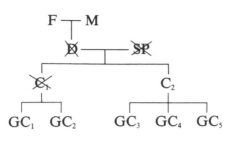

7. If you are not survived by a spouse, issue, or parents (for example, if you never married and never had children), your property goes to your brothers (B), Sisters (S), Nieces (N), Nephews (N), great-nieces, great-nephews, etc. It passes down the line of the family tree to someone who can take it.

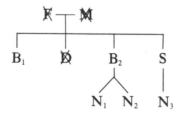

In this example, B_1, B_2, and S take one third each.

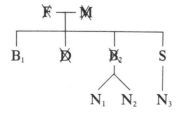

Here, B_1 and S take one third each, and N_1 and N_2 take one sixth each (they share B_2's one third).

8. If you are not survived by a spouse, issue, parents, or issue of parents, then your grandparents take your intestacy property. If your grandparents are deceased, then your intestacy property will go to their issue, that is, your aunts, uncles, cousins, etc. If none of them is alive, then your great-grandparents, and if they are deceased, their issue will take the property. Some states cut off the family tree before this; a few extend it out to your great-great-grandparents. Only if all of your extended family are deceased will your intestacy property go to your state's coffers.

There are two things to note about the intestacy laws. The first is that in most states a person has to die without any issue or parents alive in order for the spouse to take the complete estate. Usually this is *not* what married persons want. They generally want all the property of the deceased spouse to go to the surviving spouse, and then when the surviving spouse dies, they want the property to go down to the children or up to the parents. The only way to ensure this happening is to write a will. The second point is that your state does not automatically take your property if you die without a will. The state will take your property if you die intestate only if everyone on your family tree up to and including (in most states) your great-grandparents and all of their issue predecease you. Otherwise, your property will pass to some person somewhere.

A number of hidden problems may arise if your children inherit your property under the intestacy laws. Under intestacy laws your children (or grandchildren, if your children are dead) will usually take a share of your intestacy property. If they're younger than the age of majority (eighteen in most states), they are under a legal disability, and can't hold the property themselves. Who will hold it for them? Well, if your spouse is alive, she or he can act as the "guardian of the property" of your minor children. But if you and your spouse are both dead, then the probate court will appoint someone to act as the guardian of your children's property. This involves hiring a lawyer; the whole procedure will cost money and take time to accomplish. Worst of all, someone you wouldn't want, such as your spendthrift brother, may be appointed. Why? Because you didn't write a will to appoint a guardian. Furthermore, the guardian of the property will function under court supervision, reporting to the judge on what he's done with the property and its earnings. Though there are obvious benefits to this procedure, the cost of following it will come out of the children's property.

If both you and your spouse are dead, then a "guardian of the person" of each of your minor children will have to be appointed by the court. The guardian of the person is responsible for the housing, clothing, education, health, and well-being of the child. (The expenses are paid for by the guardian of the child's property.) Without a will, you will have no say in the selection of this guardian and he or she may or may not be the same person as the guardian of the property. If the two are different persons, you can only hope that they will work together for the benefit of your children.

Another problem regarding intestacy and minor children is this: your children will divide their share of your intestacy property *equally,* regardless of need or fairness. You need a will to allocate different amounts to different children.

A final consideration is that your children will take full control of their share of your intestacy property when they reach the age of majority. Will they have the necessary maturity to handle such an inheritance at that age? If not, you need a will to state at what age they should get your property.

These illustrations show how important it is that parents of minor children in particular have wills.

Let's take a breather for half a minute and remember what we're talking about here. We've discussed only two things: what property is and is not subject to the intestacy laws, and where that property goes. We have not said a thing yet about probate, and we have not said anything about taxes. We'll find out in more detail later that all the property that is subject to the intestacy laws (the "intestacy property" in the box on page 7) may indeed be subject to probate, although the "LSTC" property (in the left-hand box) probably won't be. And we will also find out that *all* the property you own, *including* the "LSTC" property, could be subject to taxes.

Here are a few sidelights to the intestacy laws. If you leave a will, then you can say in your will exactly how you want the following problems to be treated. But without a will, the following rules automatically apply.

Property located in another state. If you die intestate, real property (land and houses or buildings) in another state that is owned by you in your name alone or as a tenant in common with others is subject to the *other state's* intestacy laws. On the other hand, personal property (for example, a car or a bank account) in another state will pass in accordance with your state's laws of intestacy.

Adopted persons. Under most intestacy laws, adopted persons (children, grandchildren, etc.) share exactly the same way that natural children do. Therefore, if you have an adopted person in your family and want his or her share to be more or less than that of your other issue, you can accomplish this only by writing a will. If you don't, the adopted person will most probably be treated under the intestacy laws exactly the same as natural issue. For example, assume that a husband dies intestate, leaving a wife, two natural children, and one adopted child. Assume also that the adopted child is a bad apple, and the husband doesn't like him. Because the husband died intestate, each of the three children gets an equal amount. The husband could have written a will and disinherited the adopted child.

Illegitimate children. Assuming he or she can prove parentage, an illegitimate child is treated in most states exactly the same as children born to your marriage. If you want to disinherit an illegitimate child, you have to write a will leaving him or her nothing.

Let's take an example to put it all together. Suppose Husband and Wife have four Children, and Husband's Father is alive. Husband dies unexpectedly, without a will (he always said, "I'll get around to writing a will, but, heck, I feel fine"). Here's his family tree:

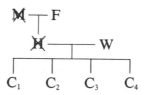

Here's a list of his property, with a note on how each asset is held:

1. house—tenants by the entirety with Wife
2. car—in his name alone
3. checking account—joint tenancy with Wife

4. furniture—he bought it all, so it's all his
5. group life insurance—Wife is primary beneficiary, and children are contingent beneficiaries.
6. savings account—in his name alone
7. investment property in Florida—title in name of Husband and three friends as "tenants in common."

Where does all this property go? Well, the house (1) and checking account (3) go directly to Wife. She also gets the life insurance (5). The intestacy laws apply to everything else. Therefore, the car, the furniture, the savings account, and the one-quarter interest in the Florida property are divided, with only a fraction (and not all) going to Wife, and the balance divided equally among Children. Chances are that Wife will feel shortchanged, because Husband always said that she'd get everything. And it was never Husband's or Wife's intent to treat Children equally: C_1 married a wealthy rock star; C_2 is a bum; C_3 needs special medical attention; and C_4 is a struggling violinist. Yet, if Wife and Children try to redistribute the intestacy property (assuming they don't squabble about who gets what), they may very well be incurring *tax* liabilities. Now *that's* news to them! See chapter 5.

WHAT'S WRONG WITH INTESTACY?

The main problem with intestacy is, of course, that you have no say where your property goes. Your spouse, your children, your adopted children, your parents—all of them may get more, or less, of your property than you might have expected or wanted. That special heirloom may go to a person that you'd rather not be the one to have it. Your funeral and burial wishes may not be carried out (will anyone know what they are?). If you and your spouse both die, so that your minor children are orphans, the court-appointed "guardian of the person" and "guardian of the property" may be people you'd rather not have watching after your children and their property. The executor of your estate may be some person you wouldn't want. Your executor and the guardian of your children's property may have to post bond, thereby costing your estate money, meaning that your heirs get less. You could end up paying a lot more in death taxes than you need to: the federal government and your state can steamroller your estate because you didn't put up any tax-savings defenses. Finally, dying intestate shows a lack of planning, meaning more than likely that your affairs will be a mess when you die. And who's left to straighten out your mess when you're gone? Your family—and at just the time when they are least able, emotionally, to do it.

How can you avoid these problems? If you didn't leave a will, then there's nothing you can do about them, and your spouse and children will have to take care of them. Why not save everyone trouble? You cared enough about your family and possessions while you were alive; don't leave them floundering when you die. The next chapter shows you what a will can do for you.

2

Your Will

ANY PERSON over the age of majority and of sound mind can make a will. The purpose of a will is to see that your property goes to those people you want it to go to, rather than to those people the state says it goes to under the intestacy laws.

Certain types of property will not pass under your will; it does not control them. Those types of property are the LSTC properties (i.e., Life insurance, Survivorship property, property in a living Trust, and your spouse's one half of the Community property). LSTC property, then, is not subject to the intestacy laws (as we have seen in chapter 1), nor is it subject to your will. What property *is* subject to your will? All property held in your name alone and your interest in property held with others as a tenant in common; also (for those in a community property state), your half of the community property and all of your separate property. In other words, the same property that was subject to the intestacy laws is subject to your will.

For example, suppose Husband is married to Wife and they have one Child. Husband leaves a valid will that says, "All my estate goes to Friend." Friend will not get any LSTC property that Husband held when he died, because it does not pass under Husband's will (unless, of course, Husband made his life insurance or his trust payable to his "estate"—something very rarely done—which his will does control). So if Husband and Wife owned their home as tenants by the entirety or as joint tenants with right of survivorship (as most married couples do), the home would go to Wife, not to Friend. If Husband had named Child as beneficiary of his life insurance policy, then the proceeds would go to Child, not to Friend. If Husband had set up a living trust to hold and manage stock while he was alive, and provided in the trust that the property be split between Wife and Child when he died, Friend would get nothing from the trust. However, any property in Husband's name alone, and his percentage interest in property held as a tenant in common with other people, will go under his will to Friend. (Since Wife has been disinherited under Husband's will, she will want to know what rights she has to get some of the property that went to Friend. Her rights against disinheritance can be called "dower," "elective share," or "forced share" rights. We'll look at Wife's rights against disinheritance later in this chapter.)

Now that you know what property your will governs, what arrangements can you make in your will? In other words, what advantages does writing a will have over intestacy? Let's look at a few points that are easy to state and then move into more complicated areas.

You can leave different amounts to different persons. As we saw in chapter I, two major difficulties with the intestacy laws are: (1) in most cases, your spouse *won't* get everything you own, and (2) your children are treated equally, whether that's fair or not. Most people in fact want their spouses to get everything, but the intestacy laws usually won't accomplish that; only a will can do it. And as to the children, the intestacy laws provide that they all get exactly the same amount, even if one needs more because of illness, educational expenses, a poor marriage, or simply because you want him or her to have more. A will can treat your spouse and children the way *you* want, not the way the state wants.

You can name specific recipients for specific items. One of the problems with intestacy is its blunderbuss approach. It gives away chunks of your estate to persons without much care as to who gets what. With a will, you can give specific items to specific persons. Your ring, the family heirloom, your automobile, the grandfather clock—all of these can go to separate persons. Moreover, you can say what happens if a recipient dies before you: "I give my opal dinner ring to my daughter, Mary, but if she does not survive me, then to my niece, Jane, if she survives me."

You can leave specific instructions regarding certain property. If you have any specific instructions regarding a particular piece of property, your will is the appropriate place for them. As an example, suppose you want your daughter to have your house when you die, but you don't want her husband to have ownership of it, since he could sell it out of the family. If you gave it outright to your daughter, she could give it to her husband or leave it to him in her will, thereby frustrating your desires. One way to avoid this situation is: "I give my house to my daughter Jane for her use during her life, and when she dies, the house is to go to my grandson James, or if he is not then alive, to my granddaughter Jill." All Jane has here is the right to use the house during her life. She couldn't sell it without James's and Jill's permission.

You can name a guardian. If you and your spouse both die before any one of your children has reached the age of majority, then that child will have to have a guardian. As discussed in chapter I, there are two types of guardians. The "guardian of the person" sees that your minor child is fed, clothed, housed, and educated. The money for these items comes from the other type of guardian, the guardian of the child's property. The "guardian of the property" is the person who holds the property that your child owns or property that you left your child under your will. The guardian of the property and the guardian of the person can be the same individual (and most people pick one person or couple for both jobs); if they are not, you should pick persons who you think will work closely together to see that your minor child is brought up correctly. Since these people have a tremendous responsibility with respect to your child and his or her property, you should think carefully about whom you want to nominate in your will. It's not always best to pick your parents—they may predecease you, or the "generation gap" may be too great. If you pick a married couple, you should be sure to state what you want to have happen with regard to your child if they get a divorce or if one of them dies. It's always wise planning to specify alternate guardians in your will. Your choice of a guardian carries great weight with the court, but your choice could be overturned if the court determines that it's in the child's best interests to do so (for example, if your named guardian develops a serious illness).

You can name your executor. In your will, you name the person who is to carry your estate through the probate process. That person is called your executor. His or her qualifications, what the job entails, and what the fee is are discussed in the next chapter. The point to be made here is that your executor controls your property and has to deal closely over a long period of time with your spouse and heirs, so the selection is a very important one. With a will you have a direct say as to who is going to administer your estate; without a will the probate judge looks at a list of people from within as well as outside your family, and it's entirely possible that someone you'd rather not have would be appointed.

You can waive a bond for your executor and your child's guardian. Because your executor will be holding and administering your money and property during probate, and because the guardian will hold and administer your child's money and property until the child reaches the age of majority, a bond may be required. A bond is a form of insurance that provides that if your executor or the guardian runs off illegally with your or your child's property, the bonding company will pay. Obviously, a bond costs money, and it is paid out of your estate or your child's property. If you have faith in the executor and guardian you name (and you should), you can provide in your will that they serve without bond, and thereby save that expense.

Funeral and burial instructions. Although you can leave a simple letter of instructions regarding your funeral and burial, a will is the traditional and appropriate place for funeral and burial directions. Even if you keep your will in a safety deposit box, in most states your executor or a family member can get it out right after your death to read these directions.

You can donate your body. If you want to leave your body, or part of your body, to a foundation or a university, for example, you may accomplish this through your will. You should also sign the appropriate forms provided by the foundation or the university.

You can provide for adopted and illegitimate children. We saw in chapter 1 that adopted and illegitimate children are treated exactly the same way your natural children are under the intestacy laws. Instead of this, in your will you can spell out just exactly what you want your adopted or illegitimate children to have.

You can disinherit. You can disinherit (that is, leave nothing to) anyone you want, including your spouse and children. But you have to be careful, because (1) they're going to want some of your estate, and (2) they may have legal rights to take some of your estate no matter what you say. This area is dangerous and complicated and is discussed in full below.

Okay, you say: "Fine. I realize how a will can help others out, but I don't have any property to worry about. What good's a will to me?" or "All my property is held jointly with my spouse. I don't need a will." Let's look at these comments separately.

The "I've got no property, so I don't need a will" person. You've probably got a lot more than you think. What about pots, pans, furniture, television set, personal effects, clothing, and jewelry? If you bought them with money you inherited

or earned in your job, then they're *your* assets and are subject
to the intestacy laws or to your will. You may have other
assets you haven't thought of. What about a rich relative who
unexpectedly leaves you property or money? Or suppose you
die because of someone else's negligence (say, in a car crash),
your executor sues the other person in a "wrongful death"
lawsuit, and collects $50,000 for your estate? And there are
other ways to "live poor, die rich." You've seen how dying
intestate can distribute your property in a manner you may
not wish. A will is a simple and inexpensive alternative that
can take care of all the property you now have and all the
property you may have when you die.

The "all my property is held jointly with my spouse" person.
First, check titles to be sure they say "joint tenants with right
of survivorship," or "tenants by the entirety." If they do not,
then if you die your spouse won't automatically take. A
description of "husband and wife," without the magic words
above, in most states creates a tenancy in common, not a
tenancy with right of survivorship.

Second, is *all* of your property held with right of survivorship? What about your household furniture? jewelry? clothing, and personal effects? Those are undoubtedly *not* held in
joint names.

Third, the problem is compounded when both spouses,
relying on the joint-ownership thinking, neglect to make
wills. Consider what happens when the surviving spouse
dies. There are no more tenants with right of survivorship
then, and so the property goes down the surviving spouse's
intestacy line. Let's take a simple example. Husband and
Wife check the deed to their home and it says, "John and
Mary Smith, husband and wife, as tenants by the entirety."
John dies. Mary gets the whole house. Now Mary dies. Who
gets the house? The answer is that it goes down her intestacy

line. If she remarried, her new husband gets his intestacy share. You think John would want that? If she didn't remarry and has no issue, that means *her* relatives take the house; John's relatives get nothing. And since it's usually not possible to know which spouse will die first, we cannot tell for sure whose relatives are going to get the house. Isn't that a sloppy way to plan your affairs?

Now let's look at a simple will, which includes most of the items talked about so far and a few new items of interest, and see how the potential problems we have raised can be easily taken care of. Please remember that the following is a "scaled-down," simplified example, and should not be used as a form. It does not contain all of the proper "legal" provisions, and is given solely for illustrative purposes. *Don't* copy it, and *don't* use it as a form!

LAST WILL AND TESTAMENT
OF
JOHN WOOD

I, JOHN WOOD, a resident of Los Angeles, California, declare that this is my Last Will and Testament, and I revoke all wills and codicils made by me before this date.

1. I direct that I be cremated, and that my ashes be scattered. In place of flowers at my funeral, I wish all cash gifts to go to the American Red Cross, Los Angeles Chapter.

2. The portrait of my father, presently located in the living room of my home, I give to my daughter Mary, if she survives me, and if she does not survive me, then to my son James, if he survives me.

3. I give the grandfather clock in the hallway of my home to my daughter Susan, if she survives me, with the hope and request that she keep the clock in the family.

4. For reasons best known to him and me, I leave my son Tom nothing under this will.

5. I give all the rest and residue of my property of whatever kind

and wherever located that I may own at the time of my death to my wife, Jane, if she survives me. If she does not survive me, then I leave all such property in equal shares to those who survive me of my children, Mary, James, and Susan. If any of those three children predecease me, then his or her equal one-third (1/3) share shall go to his or her issue, per stirpes.

6. No adopted person shall share any portion of my estate. Any child born to me after the date of this will shall share on an equal basis with Mary, James, and Susan under Article 5 above.

7. Any person who does not survive me by thirty days shall be deemed to have died before I did, and shall take nothing under this will.

8. I name my wife, Jane, as executrix of this will. If, for any reason, she is unable to qualify or ceases to act, then I name my good friend, Herbert Jones, as executor. If for any reason he, too, is unable to qualify or ceases to act, then I appoint _____ Bank and Trust Company to serve as my executor. My executor shall serve without bond.

9. If my wife does not survive me, or if she dies after my death without having made provision for the custody and care of my minor children or for the management of their property, then I appoint my sister-in-law, Barbara Smith, of Las Vegas, Nevada, as guardian of the person and of the property of any of my minor children. If for any reason she is unable to qualify or ceases to act, then I appoint my wife's brother, Henry Taylor, of Hilo, Hawaii, as guardian of the person and property of any of my minor children. Such guardians shall serve without bond.

I have signed this will, which is typewritten on two pieces of paper, on this _____ day of _____, 19____, and have also written my name at the bottom of the first page.

_____

JOHN WOOD

On the _____ day of _____, 19____, JOHN WOOD declared to us, the undersigned, that the foregoing instrument was his Last Will and Testament. He requested us to act as witnesses to it and to his signature. After having made such declaration and request, he then signed the will in our presence, we being present at the same time. Now, at his request, in his presence, and in the presence of one another, we subscribe our names as witnesses, and each of us declares that in his or her opinion, JOHN WOOD is of sound and disposing mind and memory.

s/ _____

s/ _____

s/ _____

Let's look at four provisions that this will contains that we haven't talked about yet.

First, what happens in Article 3 if Susan does not survive the testator? Where does the grandfather clock go? Notice that the testator said Susan could have the clock only if she survives him. If she does not, the grandfather clock would be disposed of under the "residue clause" that appears in Article 5. It would go to wife Jane. Likewise with the portrait of the father given away in Article 2. If Mary predeceases the testator, then it goes to James; if he predeceases the testator also, then the portrait goes under Article 5.

Second, let's look at Article 5 itself. The "residue" of the testator's estate goes to his wife, Jane. What is the "residue"? It's all the property in his name alone, or his percentage interest in any tenant-in-common property, *other than* the portrait and the grandfather clock (which were given away earlier in the will). However, from the residue is subtracted property and cash needed to satisfy debts that John owed when he died, probate costs, and death taxes payable to the federal and state governments. The amount that remains is what Jane gets.

Now, suppose Jane predeceases the testator. The will then says that Mary, James, and Susan share the residue, one third each. Suppose Susan also predeceased the testator. The will says her one-third share goes to her issue, "per stirpes." The term "per stirpes" is a frequently used term, and its meaning can best be explained by a diagram.

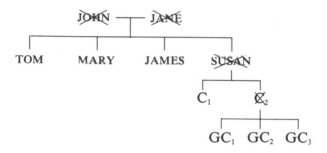

As you can see, when Susan predeceased the testator, she left one child alive and one child deceased. The deceased child had three children (who would be, of course, Susan's grandchildren). The term "per stirpes" simply means that a share filters down through succeeding generations. Therefore, C_1, Susan's child who is alive, would take half of Susan's share of one third, or one sixth, and Susan's three living grandchildren would take their parent's one-sixth share equally, or one eighteenth each. You may recall that this is usually what happened under the intestacy examples given in chapter I.

See, especially, example no. 2, on page 9. "Per stirpes" is a frequently used term because the disposition it requires is what most people want. It is to be contrasted to "per capita," under which GC_1, GC_2, GC_3, and C_1 all take an equal amount.

Third, what is the purpose behind the provision in Article 7 of John's will that requires a beneficiary to survive him by thirty days? This is really a "simultaneous disaster" provision. John is essentially saying to each of his beneficiaries that if they die in a plane or auto crash with him, or if they die within thirty days after his death (whether or not in the same accident), that he'd rather have his gift go to somebody else who can enjoy it. There is no magic in the use of thirty days. It could be one day or one year. The obvious problem with a period of time as lengthy as one year is that the beneficiary can't have the gift until one year has passed, and John's estate would have to be kept open at least that long. Thirty days, or sixty days, is usually chosen by most people as a sufficient period of time to accomplish John's objectives.

Fourth and last, what happens if the grandfather clock is sold, destroyed, or given away before John dies? Does Susan get anything? The answer is No. This is because "a will speaks at death," meaning that it becomes operative only when you die. If you don't have an asset at death, a beneficiary simply doesn't get it and can't charge your estate for it.

For many people a simple will, such as the one discussed above, will be sufficient. There are some other ideas you should know about, however, and they will be discussed in the rest of this chapter:

1. The use of trusts.

2. The rights of others to get more than you left them under your will. Suppose they don't like what they were given under the will, or suppose they were given nothing. Do

they have any legal rights to get more? Can they start a will contest? How?

3. Should you write your own will?
4. Reviewing, changing, and revoking wills.
5. Foreign wills.
6. Death with dignity.
7. Powers of attorney.
8. List of instructions for your family and executor.

TRUSTS IN YOUR WILL

What is a trust? A trust is simply an arrangement under which you give your property to somebody else and he or she holds it for you or your beneficiaries. Obviously, you will want to give the other person directions concerning how the property is to be managed, how much income you want, who gets the property when you die, what the other person's fee is for holding and managing your property, and so on. Those directions should be spelled out in a writing, called a trust agreement, to prevent misunderstandings later on. Here's a simple example of a trust. Let's say you give 100 shares of stock to Joe. You write him a letter, as follows: "Joe, here are 100 shares of stock. I'm tired of managing them. You manage them, meaning that you can trade them as you see fit, but be sure to pay me the dividends every year. I reserve the right to take back some or all of the stock at any time, and I can retract this agreement. After I die, I want my son, John, to have these shares, but not until he's twenty-five, when I think he'll be mature enough to handle them. In the meantime, pay him the dividends, but don't give him any of the stock itself. For your services in managing the stock, I agree to pay you $100 per year; you can just take it out of the dividends."

This is clearly a trust. If you gave those shares of stock and instructions to Joe while you were alive, it would be called a "living" trust. That kind of trust has many advantages, which are discussed in chapter 4. On the other hand, if you gave those shares and instructions to Joe under your will, it would be called a "testamentary" trust, because it's established under your last will and *testament.* Obviously, in a testamentary trust, Joe, the "trustee," wouldn't get the shares of stock until you die; you'd retain control until then. This section deals only with "testamentary trusts." What are some of the advantages of a testamentary trust? What can it do for you?

A testamentary trust is a substitute for an outright gift under your will. You could have given your son, John, those 100 shares outright under your will. Instead, you put them into a trust, with Joe as trustee. Here are the advantages of putting property into a trust under your will:

You can name the time the recipient is to receive the property. If you don't set up a trust under your will, then any beneficiary, including your children, will take the property when they turn eighteen, which is the age of majority in most states. You may think age eighteen is a little young for your son, John, to receive 100 shares of stock, especially if it's worth quite a bit. The advantage of a trust is that you can predetermine the age at which you want John to get those 100 shares. As shown in the previous example, you can provide that John gets only the income from the shares of stock until age twenty-five. But you can also go further and provide that if the trustee determines that John needs some of the principal (that is, the shares of stock themselves) for his health or education before he reaches twenty-five, then the trustee can distribute whatever number of shares the trustee decides is best. The trust would end when John reaches twenty-five, at which time he takes the remaining shares outright. Or, you could even stagger the time John is to receive the shares themselves. For example, you could give him one half of the shares at twenty-five and the other half at thirty. That way, if he handles the first fifty shares unwisely at twenty-five, he will have five years to regret his decision and perhaps be a little wiser when he gets the second installment at thirty.

A trust provides for competent management. An outright gift of property to a beneficiary who has poor business sense, or who is ill, or who is not competent because of young or old age could result in a fast loss of that property. For example, if John had been given those 100 shares outright, he would have every right to sell them and invest the proceeds in Peruvian nickel mines, and perhaps lose everything. A trust can provide protection for John. It can give him the benefits of those shares (income plus principal), while making sure that the shares themselves aren't all lost. So when you choose your trustee, you will want to choose someone whose management and business sense you respect. A member of the family may not be the best trustee.

A trust can keep property in your family. Take, for example, the spouse who is in a second marriage. Larry Williams had three children by his first wife. She died, and he remarried. His new wife, Nancy, is a nice lady, and he wants to provide for her if he should die first. However, if he simply gives her property outright, she may remarry or give it to someone else under her will. (This would be an equal danger if Nancy were Larry's first wife.) Larry's three children would be cut out. To resolve this, he puts his property in a trust; when he dies, the trustee pays Nancy the income from the trust property every month. Larry also authorizes the trustee to disburse whatever part of the property itself Nancy needs for her "health, support, travel, care, and comfort." If Larry thinks Nancy's rights to the principal are too liberal under those conditions, he can limit them to, for example, "health and support." (Or he can provide that she has no rights at all with regard to the principal.) Then when Nancy dies, the trust ends and the property that is remaining goes to Larry's children in whatever shares and proportions Larry has stipulated in his will. Larry has thus succeeded in both (1) providing for Nancy and (2) keeping the property in his family.

A trust can put certain restrictions on property. Suppose those 100 shares of stock we used in our earlier illustration were in a company that you owned with your brother. If you gave these shares to your son, John, outright, he might sell them, thereby allowing outsiders into your company, something your brother would not like. With a trust, you can avoid this situation by simply instructing the trustee not to give the shares to John until, say, your brother dies.

A trust can transfer property after a beneficiary dies. If you give those 100 shares of stock directly to John, and then he marries, writes a will, and dies, the chances are that he will have left those 100 shares to his wife, your daughter-in-law. They will then be out of your family's control. With a trust, you could have provided that John gets the dividends (and principal, too, if he needs it) from those shares until he dies, and when he dies, the shares themselves go down to his children. That way you, and not John, have the say on where the property goes when he dies.

A trust can give your family very significant tax savings not otherwise available. See chapter 5.

Obviously, a trust is an extremely flexible device. What it really allows you to do is to continue to call the shots even after you are dead. In doing so, it allows you to protect your loved ones, to perpetuate your wishes, and (as we'll see later) to avoid repeated payments of death taxes as family members pass away.

Let's take a look at a sample testamentary trust that Mary and Pete Miller, an elderly couple, set up for their children. Mary and Pete are married and have two children, George and Jane. Mary wants to give all her property to Pete, and Pete wants to give his property to Mary. They're both concerned about what should happen after they're both gone. How should they leave their property that would be best for their children? One possibility is to give the children the property outright. But . . . unfortunately, George is a ne'er-do-well. He already has two children, and he is not a good father to them. Moreover, Mary and Pete do not like George's wife, and are afraid that if they leave him anything outright, she may end up with it. Jane, on the other hand, is a delightful person, but her ability to manage money is questionable. Let's look at what Mary and Pete decided to do under their wills (both wills read the same way and therefore are called "reciprocal wills"). Please note that, as was true of the prior will sample (that of John Wood), this is a simplified trust form, and is not intended under any circumstances to be used by you as a form. This example does not contain some provisions found in a real testamentary trust, and is given solely for illustrative purposes. Don't copy this will, and don't use it as a form.

LAST WILL AND TESTAMENT
OF
MARY MILLER

I, MARY MILLER, a resident of Chicago, Illinois, declare that this is my Last Will and Testament, and I hereby revoke all wills and codicils made by me before this date.

1. I give all my property of whatever kind and wherever located that I may own at the time of my death to my husband, PETE MILLER, if he survives me.

2. If my husband, PETE, does not survive me, then I give all my property to ANN MUNSON, to act as trustee for the following two trusts:

A. My trustee shall take one third (1/3) of all my property and set it aside in a separate trust for my son, GEORGE. While George is alive, my trustee shall distribute to him all the net income from this trust, but no distributions of principal shall be made to George at any time for any purpose. The trustee may, however, make distributions of principal from this trust to or for the benefit of George's issue in whatever shares the trustee determines necessary or advisable for their education, health, maintenance, welfare, comfort, and travel. Distributions of principal to such issue may be unequal and need not be prorated; no distributions of principal to any issue of George shall count against any amounts such issue will receive at the termination of this trust. This trust shall terminate when George dies and his youngest child reaches twenty-one years of age. At that time, the trustee shall take the trust income and principal that is then remaining and distribute it to George's issue who are then alive, per stirpes.

B. The trustee shall take two thirds (2/3) of my property and place it into trust for the benefit of my daughter, JANE. The trustee shall pay to Jane all the net income, and whatever amount of principal the trustee decides is necessary or advisable for her health, education, maintenance, welfare, travel, and comfort. When Jane reaches the age of thirty, one half (1/2) of the assets then held in trust shall be distributed, free of trust, outright to her.

When she reaches the age of thirty-five, then the assets remaining held in trust shall be distributed outright to her. If she should die before reaching the age of thirty-five, then the assets remaining in trust shall be held in trust until her youngest living child reaches twenty years of age, and shall then be distributed to her issue then alive, per stirpes. Between her death and such time for distribution, the trustee may make, in its discretion, distributions of income and principal to any of Jane's issue who need it for education. Any such distributions will not count against the share receivable at termination.

3. Any adopted person shall be considered a natural-born person.

4. Any person who does not survive me by thirty days shall be deemed to have died before I did, and shall take nothing under this will.

5. I name _____ Trust Company to serve as my executor, without bond.

I have signed this will, which is typewritten on two pieces of paper, on this _____ day of _____, 19____, and I have also written my name at the bottom of the first page.

_____

MARY MILLER _____

On the _____ day of _____, 19____, MARY MILLER declared to us, the undersigned, that the foregoing instrument was her Last Will and Testament. She requested us to act as witnesses to it and to her signature. After having made such declaration and request, she then signed the will in our presence, we being present at the same time. Now, at her request, in her presence, and in the presence of one another, we subscribe our names as witnesses, and each of us declares that in his or her opinion, MARY MILLER is of sound and disposing mind and memory.

s/ _____

s/ _____

s/ _____

If you decide upon a testamentary trust, whom should you name as your trustee? Obviously, you should have great faith in the management and business expertise of your trustee, as well as in his or her common sense and understanding of your goals. If you decide upon a certain person, what's going to happen if that person moves from your home state, does not want the job, or dies? If you name a person as trustee, then be sure to name a successor to take over in case one of these events occurs.

What about a trust company? The good thing about a corporate trustee is that someone will always be there; the corporation's trust officers are not going to die all at once or move out of the state. Further, they are professionals in the area of property management, and devote all their time to it. The chances are that they will be bringing greater business expertise to the management of your property than a friend may be capable of. The trust companies have in-house experts on securities, bonds, money management, and real property management. Their personnel can provide, usually for free, advice on how you might realize your estate-planning objectives. They will also tell you what their fees will be for their services as trustee. Fees vary from state to state. Sometimes they are set by law; sometimes they are not and the parties can work out their own agreement. Sometimes people try to "save the fee" by naming an individual trustee. And sometimes they find they get what they pay for.

A testamentary trust does not avoid probate, its publicity, delays, or expense, since this kind of trust is set up under your will. This means that your property moves through your will, through probate, and then into the trust. The other kind of trust, the living trust, does avoid probate, and is discussed in chapter 4.

If you want to manage your own property until you die, then you can do this by setting up a testamentary trust (which is activated after you die) or a living trust in which you name yourself as your own trustee (more on this in chapter 4).

RIGHTS OF OTHERS TO TAKE MORE THAN YOU LEFT THEM UNDER YOUR WILL

To see who would have a right to take more than you left them under your will, divide all the people in the world into three groups: (1) your spouse and children; (2) any of your other heirs (i.e., those people who would take a piece of your estate if you died intestate—for example, your parents, brother, sister—see the charts in chapter 1), and anyone else you gave something to under your next earlier valid will; and (3) everyone else.

Members in each group have different rights to get more than you left them. Members in group 1 may have automatic rights to a certain share of your estate. They don't have to resort to a will contest to get that automatic share. Members in group 2 generally have no automatic rights at all, but have to resort to a will contest in court to get more of your estate. Members of group 3 have no automatic rights, and have no rights even to wage a will contest. Your estate is safe from them.

Let's look at the rights of members in group 1. First of all, what are your spouse's rights to get more than you left him or her under your will? Well, your spouse's rights can be called "dower," "elective share," or "forced share" if your spouse is a widow, and "curtesy," "elective share," or "forced share" if your spouse is a widower.

In some states a widow's rights are the same as a widower's rights; in other states there may be a preference for one sex over the other.

How much can your spouse get? In some states she or he can automatically get the same amount as if you had died intestate. In other states she or he can automatically take a fraction (one third, one half, etc.) of your real estate, and a fraction of everything else. Some states only allow her or him to use the fractional part of the real estate for her or his lifetime. And some states give your spouse a flat dollar amount (say $40,000) and a fractional share of everything else. In the community property states, the surviving spouse is protected by her or his one-half share of the community property.

Let's take an example. Many states give your spouse a right to take a fractional share of your "net probate estate." For this example, let's assume your state allows your spouse one third of your "net probate estate." What is the "net probate estate"? Let's take it in two parts. The "probate estate" is all the property that goes under your will, meaning all the property held in your name alone and your percentage interest in property held as a tenant in common with others. During the course of probate, the probate estate shrinks from a "gross" probate estate to a "net" probate estate. The next chapter explains how and why it shrinks, but for now it is sufficient to know that the following major costs will come out of your gross probate estate: funeral expenses, state and federal income and death taxes, debts you owed at your death, and the costs of probate. What's left is your "net probate estate," and your surviving spouse automatically gets one third of that. Is this complicated? If so, let's look at this example. Husband dies, and leaves a valid will that gives Wife $10,000 and provides that everything else goes to X. Husband's property, at his date of death, consists of a house held with Wife in tenancy by the entirety; a life insurance policy for $100,000 payable to his child, Sam; $100,000 in stocks in his name alone; a $5,000 automobile in his name alone; $15,000 in cash in his name in various checking and savings accounts in banks and savings and loans. Can Wife get more than the $10,000 Husband left her? That depends on her "dower" or "elective share" rights, which in this example depend on his "net probate estate." Husband's gross probate estate is $120,000. (Neither the house, which went to Wife automatically as a tenant by the entirety, nor the life insurance, which went to Sam, is in Husband's gross probate estate.) From the gross probate estate, taxes of $5,000, debts of $9,000, and probate expenses of $7,000 are subtracted, leaving a net probate estate of $99,000. Wife's elective share is one third of that, or $33,000. Since this is more than the $10,000 she was left under the will, she "elects against the will." This means that she tells the probate judge that she's not taking what the will left her, but instead is taking her elective share. Thus, she loses her $10,000 under the will, but gets her $33,000 elective share. X receives the balance of $66,000.

Suppose Wife is not satisfied with the automatic right to one third. Can she get more? In most instances Yes, but in some cases No. What happens here is that Wife wages a will contest to have Husband's will declared invalid by the probate court. If her will contest is successful, and if Husband had no previous valid will, he's declared intestate. Now, if

Wife's share of Husband's estate under the intestacy laws is more than her automatic "dower" or "elective share" amount, then she profits. If, however, her dower rights and her intestacy rights are exactly the same, then she's better off taking her automatic dower share than she is spending money to wage a will contest.

How does Wife have Husband's will declared invalid? We'll go into that very shortly, but for now you should know that your will will not be declared invalid just because you left your spouse nothing or only a pittance. There are only a few reasons why a will can be declared invalid, and leaving your spouse (or anyone, for that matter) nothing is not one of them.

What rights do your children have to take more than you left them under your will? The laws of many states divide your children into two groups, and gives the members of each group different rights.

The first group is composed of children born before you executed your will. They usually have no automatic rights to share in your estate (such as your spouse has with the elective share). You are not obliged to leave these people anything, even the proverbial "$1.00." If you intend to disinherit, however, in order to prevent an embittered child from bringing a will contest on the grounds that you lost your marbles as shown by the fact that you forgot who your children were, it's best to say simply, "I leave my daughter, Joy, nothing." Don't call your child names. Don't slander your child (or anyone else, for that matter) in your will. If you do, he or she may hold your estate liable.

Children born after the will is executed constitute the second group. In certain cases and under certain circumstances, members of this group have an automatic right to take their intestate share of your net probate estate—mean-

ing they share in your estate as if you had died intestate. The
rules governing this second group are usually a bit complex,
and to avoid them it is best simply to state directly in your
will that "no child of mine born after the execution of this
will shall share in my estate," or "any child born to me after
the execution of this will shall share in my estate equally with
all my children for whom I have left gifts under this will,"
whichever is your intent. Notice that that is what was done
in Article 6 of John Wood's simple will, which appears earlier in this chapter.

Now let's shift to the rights of those persons in group 2.
Group 2 is composed of anyone who would take something
if you had died intestate (see the charts in chapter 1). Your
spouse, children, parents, brothers, sisters, nieces, nephews,
aunts, etc.—any of them could be an heir and therefore are
members of group 2. If they are successful in a will contest,
you will be considered to have died without a valid will. The
intestacy laws would then apply, and they will be entitled to
a share of your estate. However, if you *had* an earlier valid
will, then it would come to life and your property would be
distributed under it. Therefore, also in group 2 are persons
who take part of your estate under your next earlier valid
will.

How can a successful will contest be waged? A will contestant has an uphill battle because the laws are designed, by
and large, to carry out the deceased's wishes. An "unfair" or
"unjust" will won't be invalidated just because someone feels
aggrieved. Instead, a will contestant has to prove his or her
case on one, or both, of two broad grounds: faulty execution
or lack of testamentary capacity.

With regard to faulty execution, every state has very strict
laws that set out the procedures for signing and witnessing
a will. *One* mistake in these procedures is enough to invali-

date your will. It generally doesn't matter how small the mistake is; if there has been any mistake in the signing or witnessing of your will, it's declared invalid and you will die intestate. This area is the simplest to protect against. Just get a competent, knowledgeable person to oversee the execution and witnessing of your will. This is covered in greater detail in the next section of this chapter.

On the second point, a will contestant may seek to have the probate court declare that you lacked "testamentary capacity" when you signed the will. Lack of "testamentary capacity" can mean a great number of things: it can mean that you lacked the mental capacity to know what you were doing, or that you were subject to undue influence, duress, or fraud when you executed your will. This area obviously is more difficult to protect against. Nonetheless, depending upon the type of problem (duress, fraud, etc.) that is anticipated as the basis for someone's will contest, certain precautions can be taken. If, for example, it is anticipated that a disappointed heir might bring a will contest based on senility, a good precaution might be to have a physician act as one of the witnesses to the will because he can later testify as to your soundness of mind.

The areas of execution and testamentary capacity are sufficiently complicated, and the punishment—intestacy—for error so severe, that I strongly recommend professional assistance in making and executing your will.

SHOULD YOU MAKE YOUR OWN WILL?

The answer is an emphatic No. You *can* make your own will, but you *should not*. There are a number of reasons for this. Most people want to draw their own wills in order to save the expense of having an attorney do it for them. As we are going to see, having an attorney prepare a will for you is simply not that expensive. Moreover, doing your own will can end up costing your heirs more than you saved. Why is this?

First, unless you've had experience in this area, it's difficult to envision all the problems that can arise in stating where you want your property to go. If you can't envision these problems, then you can't provide against them in your will. Let's take a simple example. Suppose you want to give your property to your children, and so you put into your homemade will: "I leave all my property to my children." This seems simple enough, but your will should also make provisions for the following contingencies: What about adopted children? What about children you do not have right now but may have in the future? Do your children take your property in equal shares, or is there some other division? What happens to the share of a child who dies before you do? Does it go to the other children who are alive? If so, does it go to them in equal shares? Or, on the other hand, does a deceased child's share go to his children (your grandchildren)? If so, does it go in equal shares? Suppose a child lives far away—does he or she have to pay for shipping expenses, or is that cost borne by all children equally?

Unfortunately, by the time these problems are first discovered, you're dead. Your will has been sent to your heirs, and someone squawks. The disappointed heir then brings a suit in the probate court asking for the court to "construe," or interpret, your will. The court can easily decide upon an interpretation you didn't really want—after all, you're dead at this time and can't tell the court what it was you intended. This entire proceeding takes time and costs money: the disappointed heir has to hire a lawyer to represent his or her side of the story, and your executor is going to have to defend your will with an attorney of his own. Court costs and attorneys' fees can quickly eat up any savings you might have realized in writing your own will.

If you do your will yourself, not only (as we've just seen) is it very possible to say things you don't mean or that others won't understand, but, far more serious, you may inadvertently cause your entire will to be invalidated. This is not too hard to do, because every state has, over the course of many years, developed rules and laws that state exactly what procedures have to be followed in making and executing a will. The law is extremely strict in this area, and leaves no room at all for error. As an example, look at what happened to Robert Williams, who died in New York in 1969. He had a wife and three adult children, but left the bulk of his $175,000 estate to some friends by his homemade will. Now, Robert was a funeral parlor director, so he thought he could do his will himself. After his death, his wife and children brought a will contest on the grounds that Robert failed to properly execute his will (there was no question that he had mental competence). The court found that Robert's will was not properly witnessed in accordance with the laws of New York, and so invalidated the will, declaring him intestate. The widow and children were victorious and, against his wishes, took his estate. The probate court had the following to say to do-it-yourselfers: "Finally, this court must note how this proceeding once again points up the disastrous results which can occur when a lay person takes it upon himself to do his own will. In this case, decedent was a young and intelligent person who was knowledgeable in death and estate matters due to his professional status as a funeral director. Nevertheless, his do-it-yourself will did not meet the requirements of law, with the unfortunate result that his intentions as expressed in the purported will were thwarted. The court cannot ignore this opportunity to warn others to seek professional legal advice and guidance before they execute such a vitally important document as their last will and testament."

A third reason for not doing your will yourself is that if you do, it's very possible that you'll end up paying a lot more taxes than you have to. That is because there are certain tax-saving plans and devices that can be put into your will. We will discuss some of these in chapter 5. Suffice it to say for the moment that the rules and regulations concerning these plans and devices are *very* technical and change very frequently. In order to get the maximum tax benefit, you have to cross every *t*, so you should see someone who is keeping abreast of the law.

Finally, someone knowledgeable in the area of estate planning can offer helpful suggestions and thoughts that perhaps had not occurred to you. An estate plan can be, and should be, tailored to fit each specific individual. There are thousands of different ways of disposing of your property, and one is going to be right for you.

Whom do you go to for assistance? Your bank, your trust company, your insurance agent, your accountant, your attorney—all of these people can assist you. Many banks and trust companies will give you professional advice for free. They have professional estate planners who will help you organize your objectives, and then assist you in selecting an attorney of your choice to polish up your plan and actually write the will and supervise its execution. What does an attorney charge for his or her services? You should remember that the amount an attorney charges is usually based on the time spent to assist you. If he spends a little time, then you will have a little bill (perhaps $75 for a simple will like John

Wood's above); if your estate is complicated and needs to be straightened out and properly put in order, then that's going to take more time and will cost you more money. However, proper planning can save you, your spouse, and your heirs a great deal of money, to say nothing of saving frustration, confusion, and emotional upheaval for your loved ones after you're gone. If you are going to do estate planning at all, you may as well do it correctly.

What do you do with your will once you have executed it? You should put the original executed copy in a safe place. Don't keep it at your house. If your house should burn up, and you with it, then your will is gone, too. You can put the original in a safety deposit box, or leave it at your attorney's office, or store it at a trust company (usually for free if they are named as trustee or executor). You can take copies home with you for your records.

REVIEWING, CHANGING, AND REVOKING YOUR WILL

First of all, a will is always drawn as if you were going to die tomorrow. That makes your decisions easier, because your property and your beneficiaries are well set in your mind, and you're not bothered by the "what ifs": "What if son Joe goes to medical school; what if daughter Sue marries wealthy; what if Dad dies and leaves me a lot of money?" If any of these things *does* happen later on, you can make adjustments to your will at that time.

Consequently, you should review your will whenever there is a major change in family circumstances, such as marriage, divorce, birth, adoption, or death. You should also review it whenever there is a major change in your assets. Tax planning may be necessary if your assets increase in value dramatically, and may be eliminated if they decrease dramatically. In any case, you should review your will every three to five years just to make sure it still says what you want it to say.

How do you change your will? *Never* change your will by marking on the original. The reason for this is that any change to a will must be executed with the same procedures as were followed for the execution of the original will. A simple line through a name or the addition of a figure is not legal without those procedures. Consequently, the only proper way to change your will is by writing a "codicil," a short amendment to your will. You should have an attorney assist you in preparing it and supervising its execution. For making major changes in your will, a codicil is satisfactory, but most people simply make a brand-new will. The new will should state expressly that it revokes the prior will. (Review the first sentence of John Wood's will, which "expressly revokes all wills and codicils I have made before this date.")

Suppose you want to revoke, rather than change, your entire will. How do you do it? There are two ways. The first way is to simply write a new will and provide, as John Wood did, that the new will "expressly revokes" all prior wills. This is the best way to do it. Destruction is the second way to revoke your will. But this method can lead to big problems. You can revoke a will by destroying it, but the catch is that when you commit the *act* of destruction you must have the *mental intent* of revoking the will and all its provisions. Therefore, an accidentally burned will is still legally valid: since the testator didn't have the intent to destroy it, it remains valid. The same is true if the testator later decides, "Oh well, I didn't want that will anyway." Since the act and the intent did not occur together, the will remains valid, and a copy of that will may be probated. You can see how a beneficiary who had a gift under a will that was later destroyed by the testator might cause trouble. He simply comes into probate court and says, "The testator never really *intended* to destroy the will. I'm going to prove that he *accidentally* threw it into the fire." In order to avoid the questions that always arise when a will is physically destroyed, it is best simply to revoke it by a subsequent written will.

FOREIGN WILLS

Wills that were executed in another state or in another country by a person who later moves to your state are considered foreign wills and may be valid in your state. Most states have laws that say wills are valid within their borders if, when they were executed, they were executed in accordance with the laws of the other state or the other country. Let's take an example. The State of California allows "holographic wills." A holographic will is a will that is entirely in the handwriting of the testator, signed by him, and dated by him. It has no witnesses. Another state, say, Hawaii, would not allow this kind of will if it was written by a Hawaii resident, because it doesn't have the witnesses required by Hawaii law. However, if the holographic will complied with the law of the State of California when it was written, then even though Hawaii would not allow that kind of will to be written by a Hawaii resident, it will accept that kind of will from a person who wrote the will while a resident of California, moved to Hawaii, and then died there.

To be sure your foreign will will be accepted in the state you reside in, you should have an attorney review it. If it's not accepted, then, of course, you die intestate.

POWERS OF ATTORNEY

Powers of attorney can be extremely useful. A power of attorney is an authorization by you to allow some other person, called your "attorney in fact," to transact business for you and in your name while you are alive. A "limited" or "special" power of attorney authorizes the attorney in fact to act for you only in a limited capacity—say, to sell your house or to sell your car. A "general" power of attorney authorizes the attorney in fact to act for you in any business transaction at all.

It is important to know right away that a power of attorney is not a will. It does not dispose of any property when you die. The authority of the attorney in fact to act for you dies when you die. A power of attorney is not valid after your death.

Powers of attorney can be extremely useful for those persons who are concerned about their own possible loss of mental competence in the future. If a person becomes incompetent to transact business for himself or herself, then obviously somebody has to do it for him. Someone has to take control of the incompetent's property. One way of getting authority to do this is through the probate court. The probate court deals not only with deceased individuals but also with the property of people who are incompetent. A "guardianship proceeding" would have to be started in the probate court. This involves publicity, hiring a lawyer, delays, and expense. It will also require the guardian of the incompetent person to file an accounting in the court as often as once every year. The reason for this is that the court wants to make sure that the guardian is not running away with the assets of the incompetent person. Every time the accounting is filed an attorney must be hired to present the accounting to the court, and this will cost money.

The second way for the person to get authority to act for the incompetent individual is to have a power of attorney, executed by the incompetent (obviously) before he or she became incompetent. We have already seen that this authorizes one individual to act for another individual. If you prepared a power of attorney before you became incompetent, then you would not need a guardianship proceeding in the probate court (except in some states, where incompetency revokes a power of attorney). This seems clear, but suppose that while you're competent you want to maintain full control of all of your assets and don't want anyone else to have his hand or nose in your business. This is very simple to accomplish in most states. You write what is known as a "standby" power of attorney. In your power of attorney, you put a provision that says, "This power of attorney shall not become effective until I become mentally incompetent to carry on my business affairs, as attested to in a writing by a licensed medical practitioner." With this kind of power of attorney, you retain 100 percent control of your assets until you become incompetent. When you do become incompetent, the power of attorney becomes effective, and your agent can act for you until you die.

DEATH WITH DIGNITY

As of this writing, the legislatures of most states have not passed any law regarding "death with dignity," that is, a law that can limit the medical measures taken to save your life.

But it is possible for an individual to write a "living will," which, at the present time, expresses only your wish, meaning that your physician is not required to honor it. Here's a sample "living will":

LIVING WILL

To my family, my physician, my clergyman, my attorney:

If the time comes when I can no longer take part in decisions for my own future, let this statement stand as the testament of my wishes:

If there is no reasonable expectation of my recovery from physical or mental disability, I request that I be allowed to die and not be kept alive by artificial means or heroic measures. Death is as much a reality as birth, growth, maturity, and old age—it is the one certainty. I do not fear death as much as I fear the indignity of deterioration, dependence, and hopeless pain. I ask that drugs be mercifully administered to me for terminal suffering even if they hasten the moment of death.

This request is made after careful consideration. Although this document is not legally binding, you who care for me will, I hope, feel morally bound to follow its mandate. I recognize that it places a heavy burden of responsibility upon you, and it is with the intention of sharing that responsibility and of mitigating any feelings of guilt that this statement is made.

DATED: _____

_____
Signed

_____
Witness

Copies have been distributed to:

_____

_____

_____

_____

(examples: immediate family, attorney, trustee, clergyman, physician)

LETTER OF INSTRUCTIONS

After you have written your will, it is a good idea to leave a handwritten (or typed) letter of instructions to your executor and family. This letter would tell them things they might otherwise not know or which would take some time in discovering. Here's a sample:

LETTER OF INSTRUCTIONS

My advisers: Attorney: _____
Insurance agent: _____
Accountant: _____
Stockbroker: _____
Investment adviser: _____
Bank officer: _____

My records: *Item*   *Located at*
Will
Securities
Insurance policies: life
home
car
health

Receivables
Mortgages
Deeds
Safety deposit box
Checkbooks
Savings deposit books
Income tax records
Trust agreements
Marriage certificate

Names and addresses of my relatives:
Names and addresses of my beneficiaries:
Others to contact in case of my death:
Social Security number:
Burial instructions:

This letter should be given to your executor, and a copy kept
with your copy of your will.

3

Probate

REGARDLESS OF whether you die with or without a will, your estate may have to be probated. There are nine different areas to understand about probate:

1. What is it—briefly?
2. Why do we need it?
3. Does everybody need it?
4. Who are the principal players in probate?
5. How does it work—in more detail?
6. Advantages of probate.
7. Costs.
8. Delays.
9. Publicity.

Let's take these areas one by one.

WHAT IS IT—BRIEFLY?

When you die, either with or without a will, certain things have to be done with your property. Someone has to collect your assets, pay your bills, pay your death taxes, and distribute your property to your beneficiaries, whom you have named under your will, or to your heirs, who receive your property under the laws of intestacy. If someone does this for you without the supervision of the probate court, then you have a simple "family settlement" and the probate judge will never need to know that you died. On the other hand, if, as in certain cases, your property cannot be dealt with or distributed without the supervision of the probate court, then, instead of a simple family settlement, you have a "probate." Therefore, the term "probate" simply means a *court-supervised* collection of your assets, payment of your bills, payment of your death taxes, and distribution of your property to your beneficiaries or heirs.

WHY DO WE NEED IT?

Say you die owning a car, or a house, or a bank account, or stock certificates or account in your name alone. These items of property are recorded in your name alone as owner—at the bank, the Division of Motor Vehicles, the land recording office, or your stockbroker's office. Obviously, title to that property cannot remain in your name after you're dead: it has to be transferred into the name of someone who is alive so that person can then own the property. But, as you might suspect, the people at those institutions are not going to change the ownership of those items into the name of someone else until they have proof positive that they can do so. This is simply for their own protection. Therefore, to get "clear title" to that land, bank account, car, or stocks, there has to be some kind of process to get the title out of your name and into the name of someone else. There may be many people who think they should have the property after you pass away. There may be competing claims. A major purpose of a probate is to resolve those competing claims to the property and to settle the title in the name of the correct person or persons.

DOES EVERYONE NEED IT?

No, because not all property has to be probated. The LSTC property (Life insurance, Survivorship property [held in joint tenancy or tenancy by the entirety], property held in a living Trust, and your spouse's one half of the Community property) avoids probate completely. Only property that you held in your name alone, or your interest in property you held as a tenant in common with other persons, *may* need to be probated. This property is called your "probate property" or your "probate estate."

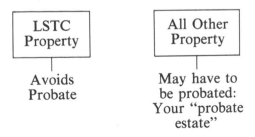

LSTC Property	All Other Property
Avoids Probate	May have to be probated: Your "probate estate"

If the property in your probate estate has no recorded title to it (such as furniture, furnishings, clothing, personal effects, and so on), then a family settlement, rather than a court-supervised probate, will be sufficient in most cases to pay your creditors, pay your death taxes, and distribute the property to your beneficiaries or heirs. The "title-clearing" function of probate, discussed above, is not required in this case. On the other hand, if property in your probate estate has a recorded title (land, a house, a condominium, a bank account, a car, etc.), then a probate is required to transfer the title into the names of your beneficiaries or heirs.

You should now have a general idea of when, and why, a probate is required. This will apply to you whether you die with or without a will. In either case, the "title-clearing" function of probate may be required to get your property into the hands and into the names of your beneficiaries.

From this point on through the rest of this chapter, we are going to assume that when you die, a probate, and not a simple family agreement and settlement, is either required to clear title or is desired for some other reason— for example, if the members of your family can't agree among themselves as to who should get what property and want the probate court to make that determination for them. So the rest of this chapter will assume that for one reason or another, your estate is going to be probated.

WHO ARE THE PRINCIPAL PLAYERS IN PROBATE?

There are really three individuals and one group of persons who make up the principal players. They are your executor, the attorney for your executor, the probate judge, and your heirs and beneficiaries.

Let's look at these people one by one to see, in a general way, what parts they play in a probate.

Your executor. We'll see in detail in the next section exactly what his job entails, but for the time being, you should know that in general the job of the executor is to be in charge of your probate. The executor collects your assets, safeguards them, pays your creditors and taxes, and then distributes your remaining assets to your beneficiaries or heirs. Since the executor is dealing with your assets during the course of probate, he or she is personally liable, of course, if the assets should be lost, stolen, burned, or wasted, or if they go to somebody they shouldn't have gone to.

How does your executor qualify for this job? If you write a will, you can name your executor. Some states prohibit certain persons (for example, non–state residents) from serving. If you do not want to name an individual as your executor, you can name a bank or trust company. Again, different states have different rules on which banks and trust companies can qualify. Your attorney can easily advise you on these points.

Any executor you name can resign before being appointed, or can resign at any point after being appointed. If your named executor resigns, or can't qualify for any reason (for example, he dies or becomes disabled), or if you have failed to name an executor in your will, or if you died intestate, then the judge will appoint somebody to act as your executor from the following list, in the following order: your surviving spouse, your children, other heirs, any of your creditors.

So whom should you choose as your executor? Should it be your spouse? Your child? A corporate trust company? A combination of the two (for example, your spouse and a corporate trust company)? These decisions are best left to you, but a brief review of the next section of this chapter will indicate to you that the jobs of an executor can be extremely time-consuming and frustrating (if your executor is inexperienced), and can lead to personal liability. In the course of probate, your executor deals closely with your heirs, your beneficiaries, your employer, your insurance companies, his attorney, the probate court, and the tax authorities. The "personal touch" is as important as a good business head. What many testators do is to name one or more individuals (such as a spouse and a child) as well as a corporate trust company in an attempt to have the best of both worlds: the trust company does all the accounting, tax returns, and "dirty work" involved, while the individual executor can lend the necessary personal touch.

The attorney for your executor. Probate can be time-consuming and complicated. An attorney is frequently indispensable to assist your executor. If your probate estate goes before the probate judge (and it may not have to—see the next section of this chapter), your executor will have to have an attorney to represent him and your estate in court. The attorney works closely with your executor in probating your estate, prepares all court filings and petitions, and ensures that your estate gets probated according to the law. The attorney will be chosen by your executor; you can name an attorney in your will, but your executor can override your choice. If an attorney is required, then obviously the attorney will have to be paid, and he will be paid out of your estate.

The probate judge. The probate judge oversees the entire probate process, and the judge's staff individually reviews all the "petitions" and filings of your executor. (A "petition" is merely a request by your executor to be allowed to do something—for example, to settle a claim against your estate.) If the judge has questions regarding any statements made in any of the petitions that the attorney files with the court, then a "hearing" may be required. This is simply a meeting wherein your executor, his attorney, and the judge get together to discuss any problems that have come up in your probate. The judge will then make a ruling, and your probate will continue on its way. The probate judge and his staff carefully review the petitions and filings in each probate to make sure that it is progressing according to the requirements of law. The judge and his staff are ordinarily paid by the state and not by your estate.

Your heirs and beneficiaries. Your "heirs" are those people who would take your property if you died intestate (review chapter 1); your "beneficiaries" are those people whom you have named to take your estate under your will. Your heirs and your beneficiaries, obviously, can be quite different persons. Your heirs and beneficiaries will be notified by your executor throughout the course of probate regarding what he's doing. Many (but not all) of the documents and petitions that your executor files in the probate court have to be sent by law to your heirs and beneficiaries. It is this publicity feature of probate that many people do not like.

When do your beneficiaries or heirs get paid the amount they get either under your will or under the intestacy laws? That happy day does not come until the absolute end of probate, and the end of probate is not going to come until many steps have been taken by your executor. Those steps are discussed in the next section of this chapter.

HOW DOES IT WORK—IN MORE DETAIL?

There are five major steps that are taken in probate: presenting your will for probate (or having you declared intestate); appointing your executor; collecting, inventorying, and safeguarding your probate assets; paying your debts and taxes; distributing the balance of your probate estate to your heirs or beneficiaries. These steps will be taken in any one of the two types of probate that are available in most states: "small estates" and "formal probate." Your executor may have a choice between the two types.

Small estates. The small estates method of probate is available in some states only if your probate estate (meaning, to repeat, the property that is going through probate, which would therefore exclude jointly held property with a right of survivorship, life insurance proceeds, property held in a living trust and your spouse's one half of the community property) is less than a certain dollar amount, say, $30,000. No executor is usually needed to take your property through Small Estates. No attorney is needed. The Small Estates department of the state court system does all the work for you. Its charge is generally nominal, plus any costs of advertising, mailings, etc. Most of the steps that they will take in

Small Estates are similar to the steps of a formal probate, which are examined in more detail below.

Formal probate. A formal probate is a probate done with an executor, an attorney for the executor, and a probate judge. Most people have formal probates.

What are the steps in a formal probate? This will get a little bit lengthy. If you have insomnia, this is the section for you. Remember, these are the steps that your executor and his attorney will have to undertake on behalf of your estate. Your choice of an executor and an attorney (you can nominate both in your will) should be people who you feel can undertake these responsibilities for the ultimate benefit of your beneficiaries. Here are the steps taken in most states. Obviously, there may be some local variations, but if so, they will probably be in terminology rather than procedure.

1. You die.

2. Right after you die, your family should secure your will. (Even if it's in your safety deposit box, it can usually be removed for the purpose of determining your funeral and burial wishes, as well as discovering whom you named as executor.) Your family should then notify your executor. Your executor may then take initial steps for securing your property, turning off the electricity and telephone, canceling newspaper and magazine subscriptions, notifying your banks of your death, and notifying your employer. At this point the executor does not want to take any further steps, simply because he's not yet officially been appointed by the probate judge. If the executor starts distributing property and paying off creditors before he is even appointed, such actions could have very unfortunate results if he is not appointed later.

Notice that no property has yet been distributed to any of your heirs or beneficiaries. In fact, if any of your family or family "friends" come in and take your property after you die, they may be doing so illegally, because it doesn't yet belong to them. There are many steps to be taken, and many persons to be paid, before your property gets to your heirs and beneficiaries.

3. Your executor can assist your family in preparing for your funeral and burial.

4. A Petition for Probate is prepared. Actually, the attorney for the executor prepares this document, the executor signs it, and then the attorney files it with the probate court. Along with the Petition for Probate is filed your death certificate (to prove that you have actually died) and the original signed copy of your will.

The Petition for Probate asks the judge to declare that your will is valid and unrevoked so that your property can go in accordance with that will to your beneficiaries. Obviously, if you have no will, then the Petition for Probate would ask the judge to declare that in fact you died intestate, and that your property should go in accordance with the intestacy laws. The second thing the Petition for Probate asks is that the judge name your permanent executor. It is important to note that not until step 7 (the hearing) will the person who has been fulfilling the job of executor be legally named as your executor, and that's the reason he or she has not done anything too dramatic with your property.

5. Newspaper notice. After the Petition for Probate is filed in the probate court, a notice is placed by your executor in the newspaper. Here's a sample of such a notice:

FIRST CIRCUIT COURT NOTICE AND NOTICE TO CREDITORS
P. NO. 12345

ESTATE OF ALLEN MUNSON, Deceased

FILED a document purporting to be the Last Will and Testament and First Codicil thereto of the above-named decedent, together with a Petition praying for probate thereof and issuance of Letters to ANN LEE and CALVIN JOHNSON, whose address is 124 Kensington Avenue, Arlington, Virginia.

Friday, June 8, 1981, at 9:00 A.M., before the Presiding Judge in Probate, in his courtroom, Judiciary Building, is appointed the time and place for proving said Will and hearing all interested persons.

All creditors of the above-named estate are hereby notified to present their claims with proper vouchers or duly authenticated copies thereof, even if the claim is secured by mortgage upon real estate, to said nominee, at the address shown above, within four months from the date of the first publication of this notice or they will be forever barred.

DATED: Apr. 20, 1981.

This notice has four separate and distinct functions. First, the notice tells people in the general public that you have died and that your executor is asking the court, in the Petition for Probate, to be named as permanent executor. Second, the notice tells the general public that the executor has presented a will to the court which the executor is asking the judge to declare is valid and unrevoked. (Alternatively, if there was no will, then the notice would state that the executor was trying to have you declared intestate.) Third, the notice tells the general public that there will be a hearing on such and such a date in the courthouse in order for the judge to review the Petition for Probate, name someone as executor, and to declare either that you have died with a certain will in full force and effect or that you have died intestate. If there is going to be a contest to try to keep your temporary executor from becoming named permanent executor, or if there is going to be a contest regarding the validity of your will (remember Howard Hughes?), or if there is going to be a contest to try to show that you did not die intestate but in fact had a will, then the best time for that contest is going to be at the hearing on the Petition for Probate. (These items of protest can be brought up later in the course of probate, but generally they're brought up at the first hearing.)

The fourth thing that the newspaper announcement does is that it gives notice to creditors that you have died and that they have a certain number of months (usually from three to six, depending on your state's laws) from the date of the first publication of that notice to present their claims against your estate. If a creditor does not present his claim against your estate within the set period, then your executor is not authorized to pay that claim out of your estate, and the creditor may have lost all his legal rights against you, your estate, and your heirs and beneficiaries. Therefore, creditors have to be eagle-eyed and review the notices in the paper every day in order to avoid missing the notice to creditors. If a creditor does spot the "Notice to Creditors" in the paper, then he will file a claim with the executor for the amount he believes you owe him. The executor then reviews the claim of the creditor and, if it is valid, pays it. The executor may, of course, reject the claim, and if he does, then the creditor can ask the probate judge to review the denial of his claim. But what happens if a creditor does not file his claim within the set period? Then, as explained above, your executor may not pay the claim. If he does, he is personally liable, and your heirs and beneficiaries can collect from him. What often happens, as you might suspect, is that the creditor who has not filed on time tries to get the sympathy of the heirs and beneficiaries in order to get their approval that he should be paid. If they approve, the creditor can be paid, since the money is ultimately coming out of their pockets.

6. Mailed notice to heirs and beneficiaries. Not only is a notice put in the paper regarding your death and the Petition for Probate, but your executor (in most states) has the duty to send a copy of the Petition for Probate *and* a copy of your will to each of your beneficiaries and heirs. Therefore, each of your heirs and beneficiaries will know exactly what's in your will as well as who's trying to be appointed as executor. This can be a touchy point, because some of your heirs may discover that they have not been named as beneficiaries. A disappointed heir can bring a will contest or express bitterness toward your beneficiaries. It is this type of publicity that is not loved by many people, and it is those people who try to avoid probate (see chapter 4).

7. The hearing for probate. About six weeks after the Petition for Probate is filed, the probate judge has a hearing that the executor and his attorney attend. The six-week delay is caused, first, because of the usual requirement that the notice be published for three or more consecutive weeks, and, second, because of the usually crowded court "calendar" (schedule).

To this hearing for probate may come any contestants who have either received notice directly (under step 6) or read about your death and the probate in the paper (under step 5). Under normal circumstances there is no contest, and in the absence of any objections the judge will appoint your permanent executor, and will "admit your will into probate." That phrase simply means that the judge declares that the document attached to the Petition for Probate is legally your valid last will and testament, and that the beneficiaries it names are the people who will take your estate after all the creditors and taxes are paid. If you died intestate and no one presented a "newly found will" at this hearing, the judge would declare you officially intestate (to the glee of your heirs). Finally, the judge will determine whether your executor has to post bond—usually, if your will states that no bond is required, the judge won't demand one.

8. Letters testamentary. Right after the hearing on probate, the judge will sign "letters testamentary," which authorize your executor to act in your place. These letters are the "keys" with which the executor can unlock any property held in your name alone; these letters give him authority to act in your place with your property. Therefore, for example, armed with these letters, your executor can go to your bank and close out the checking account that is in your name. Of course, without the letters, the bank would never release the funds to your executor. Since one of his duties is to preserve your estate's assets and to make them productive, he'd set up a savings account in his name as executor and deposit your money there.

9. Administering your probate property. Now that your executor has the letters testamentary and has been officially appointed, he can begin to assemble, safeguard, and inventory your property. Here are some of the jobs he will now undertake. The post office should be notified to forward your mail to the executor; the family should send him your bills. The executor collects all income, receivables, and other monies due you or your estate. Since your estate will have this income coming in, it may have to pay a federal and state income tax, called a "fiduciary income tax." (Your executor must apply with the federal government to get a federal ID tax number for the fiduciary tax return.) Your safety deposit box should be located, and its contents inventoried. A bank

account should be opened by the executor for your estate. Your real estate must be insured, safeguarded, and managed. All valuables must be safeguarded—if no one else is home, by removing them from your property and placing them in a vault. Claims for veteran's, fraternal, lodge, union, social security, and other death benefits should be made. And since no matter when you died, you lived at least a part of the year, federal and state income tax returns will have to be filed and a tax may have to be paid.

Finally, your executor must be a bookkeeper as well. That's because throughout the course of probate he'll have to keep accounts itemizing income and disbursements. Whenever any interest, dividends, rents, insurance refunds, or any other cash or property comes into your estate, your executor should note that in his accountings; similarly, any time he makes any payments out of your probate estate (for example, for your debts, taxes, the executor's and attorney's fees, court filing costs, etc.), he should note those. Your executor can hire an accountant to do this for him, but that will cost money that comes out of your estate. At the end of the probate these accountings are put together and submitted to the court for its review and approval.

10. Inventory. After the hearing for probate (step 7), your executor must file with the court an inventory of all assets that are being probated, that is, all assets in your probate estate. If there is any property that has not yet been appraised, the court may order an appraiser to determine the value of such property. The fee for the appraisal can be expensive, and of course your estate pays. Why is an appraiser needed? Because your executor will pay your federal and state death taxes based upon the appraised value of your property, and no one's going to take your executor's word for how much your property is worth.

11. Payment of creditors. Meanwhile the period for creditors, which started back in step 5, is running. After the period has run and your executor is certain that he has all the claims that he is going to have, then he will review the claims and make payment of those he determines are valid. But what happens if there isn't enough money in your "probate estate" to pay off all your creditors? Then your creditors get paid off, usually in something like the following order: the fees of your executor and the attorney for your executor come out first; reasonable funeral expenses come out second; "family allowance" comes out third; "homestead allowance" comes out fourth; "exempt property" comes out fifth (these terms are defined in step 14); taxes come out sixth; medical and hospital expenses of your last illness come out seventh; other claims come out eighth. If your executor has to sell any of your probate property—including your home if that's in the probate estate—in order to pay your creditors, then he will do so. You will notice that not until all eight steps of creditors are paid off *completely* will your heirs or beneficiaries take anything from your probate estate. They are in the unnamed ninth bracket. If your estate cannot pay off all eight levels of creditors, then you have an "insolvent" estate, and your heirs and beneficiaries will definitely receive nothing out of your probate estate.

12. State inheritance tax. Your executor and the attorney for your executor will prepare a state inheritance tax return, which your executor will sign and then file with the state. This is discussed in more detail in chapter 6, but the point to be made here is that your probate cannot close until this return has been filed, the tax paid, and a receipt filed in court.

13. Federal estate tax. Again, your executor and the attorney for your executor will prepare the return for your federal estate tax, your executor will sign the return, and it will be

filed. The federal return, and any tax due, are due nine months after the date of death; the state inheritance tax return, and any tax due, are ordinarily due sometime after that. Extensions for both returns may be granted for good reasons.

14. Maintaining the family during probate. You have seen already that no heir or beneficiary can take any of your estate until all the steps mentioned in this section are completed and your estate is closed. It should be getting clear that it takes a long time to close an estate. What happens to your family in the meantime? Aren't they allowed to get any money out of your estate in order to feed, clothe, house, and educate themselves until your estate is closed? Well, we saw in section 11 that certain rights, called homestead allowance, exempt property, and family allowance, come very high in the order of items to be paid. (Different states have different names for these rights, such as "spouse's allowance," "children's allowance," "maintenance provisions," and so on.) These types of allowance allow the executor to make payments to your family while probate is progressing, assuming your probate estate has enough in it to pay your executor, his attorney, and your funeral bills (which are ordinarily the first two rungs of creditors). All other creditors—even taxes—in most states come *after* these allowances. Let's assume that there is enough money in your estate to pay off the first two rungs of creditors, so that your family will have some rights, ahead of all other creditors, to receive money and property out of your probate estate before it actually closes. What are those rights?

The purpose of these rights is to maintain your family during the long course of probate. The laws vary from state to state, but most states have laws that provide something like the following. First, your spouse and minor children are entitled to a reasonable "family allowance" in money out of your probate estate while the probate is progressing. The judge will decide how much is "reasonable" for your family after a hearing. This allowance can be paid in a lump sum or in periodic installments. Ordinarily, it will be limited in duration or amount if your probate estate is not able to pay other claims. The second right is the right to a "homestead allowance." The homestead allowance gives a fixed dollar amount to your spouse, or if there is no surviving spouse, then to all of your minor and dependent children as a group. Often, the "homestead" right allows your family to live in your home temporarily, even if it ultimately goes to someone else under your will. Third, in addition to the family allowance and homestead allowance, your spouse may have a right to "exempt property." This means that your surviving spouse (or if he or she is not alive, then all of your children as a group) has the right to take a certain dollar amount's worth of household furniture, automobiles, furnishings, appliances, and personal effects.

Two additional comments on family support during probate: Note that even if your family won't ultimately get your probate estate (say, because your will left it all to a distant cousin), they still have these three rights to allowances, and the money and property goes to them before it goes to that distant cousin. Second, your family will already have received any life insurance, survivorship property, or property held in a living trust. All we've been talking about here is your family's rights to get at your *probate* estate during the lengthy course of probate.

15. Petition for distribution of estate and presenting final accountings. This is the final petition that the attorney for the executor will prepare and your executor will sign. It tells the judge that all creditors have been paid to the extent the

probate estate was able to pay them, that your state inheritance taxes have been paid, and that your executor is ready to pay the remaining property to your beneficiaries or heirs. Attached to this petition are the accounts of the executor, which he has been keeping during the course of your probate. If your estate has been open a long time, or if the accounts are confusing or exceptionally lengthy, the court's staff may not have the opportunity to review them itself. In this case the judge will appoint a "master," who is an attorney, to review the executor's accountings to be sure that all payments have been properly made and all receipts have been properly accounted for. The master will charge a fee for his services, which will be paid out of your estate. In order to avoid the appointment and cost of a master, your executor may ask your beneficiaries or heirs to review his accounting. What the heirs and beneficiaries are really reviewing and approving is the final, net amount that remains in the probate estate after the executor has done all the steps noted above. If they are content with this figure, and the accounting process by which it was arrived at, they approve the account. If they are not content with this figure or the accounts, or think that the executor has been remiss in any of his duties, they do not approve the accounts and will probably request the probate court to review the accounts via a master.

16. Notice in newspaper. At this point, ordinarily a second notice must be placed in the newspaper that tells the general public that the executor is going to close the probate and distribute to the beneficiaries or heirs the property that remains. If any member of the general public (such as a creditor who has not yet been paid) has any objections or complaints, then they can attend the hearing, the time and date of which is indicated in the newspaper notice.

17. The hearing. At the hearing the judge reviews the

petition for distribution, has reviewed (or has had a master review) the executor's accountings, and, if everything is in order, authorizes the executor to close the probate and distribute the remaining property either to the beneficiaries under your will or to your heirs at law. The property will be delivered to them *in their names:* therefore, title has gone from you to your executor during probate and to your heirs or beneficiaries at the end of probate. Thus, one of the main functions of probate—title clearing—is now complete. The judge also tells the executor that after he has distributed the property and collected receipts from the heirs or beneficiaries, his job is complete and he no longer has any duties as executor. Your probate is, at last, finished.

Having seen the complications in probate, you may ask the question: What are the *advantages* to having your estate probated?

ADVANTAGES OF PROBATE

Court supervision. Every step of the probate process is reviewed and overseen by the probate court. Nothing is left to chance or to greedy relatives. Everyone gets what he or she is entitled to under the laws of intestacy or under your will.

The creditor claim period. Without a probate your creditors can haunt your heirs or beneficiaries for a lot longer than the few-month period that probate allows them. Many estates are probated solely to take advantage of this "claim now, or forever hold your peace" provision.

Title clearing. Probate clears title to all titled property out of your name and into the names of your heirs or beneficiaries.

If these are the advantages of probate, what are its *disadvantages?*

COSTS

Let's remember that whether or not your estate goes through probate, there are going to be many costs and expenses. Funeral costs, state and federal income taxes, state and federal death taxes, appraisers' fees, and payment of all your creditors constitute some of the major outlays of money whether you die with or without a probate estate. So the appropriate question with regard to probate is: What does it cost to probate your estate that it wouldn't cost if you avoided probate? Well, there are two major costs: your executor's fee for his or her work, and the attorney's fee for his or her work helping your executor. How much will these fees be?

Probate fees vary widely from state to state. Most states have laws setting the fee at a certain percentage (or sliding percentage) of the "gross" probate estate or the "net" probate estate (i.e., the gross probate estate less any debts or mortgages). Some states allow additional fees for work on assets outside the probate estate (such as LSTC property); some states allow "extraordinary" fees for extraordinary work, such as preparing income or death tax returns, selling a piece of real estate during the probate, or continuing to operate the business of the dead person. Some states give the attorney for the executor exactly the same fee they give the executor; other states require the executor and his attorney to prove the worth of their services by such criteria as time spent, results obtained, difficulty of the job, experience required. Some states allow the executor and sometimes the attorney to charge a minimum fee.

A "ballpark" figure that is often given (obviously, subject
to variation from state to state) is that the executor will
charge about 2 percent of the probate estate for his work and
the attorney the same, and that an additional 1 percent will
be spent for newspaper publication(s), mailing, duplication,
and court filing costs. Thus, if you figure your probate will
cost about 5 percent of what is going through probate, you
probably won't be too far wrong. However, it may cost more
than that: many states have sliding fee schedules that start
at a higher percentage rate and then decrease as the value of
the probate estate increases. Thus, if you have a relatively
"small" probate estate, it may cost 10 percent or more, rather
than 5 percent, to get through probate.

Probate, obviously, is not cheap, but remember that your
executor and his attorney have done a great deal of work, for
which, naturally, they should be paid.

DELAY

The fact is that it will take at least nine months to probate
even the simplest estate. More complex estates can take a *lot*
longer. Some delays are built into the system: the several-
week period for newspaper notice both at the start and at the
end of probate; the creditor-claim period; the fact that the
federal death-tax return is due nine months after death, and
is seldom filed earlier than that. Other delays are caused by
the clogged court calendar, and by the sheer number of
duties that your executor and his attorney have to undertake.

An "average" probate takes one to one and one-half years
to complete. There's little, if anything, that can be done to
speed things up. Your heirs or beneficiaries are going to have
to wait before they get your money.

PUBLIC NOTICE

We've seen already that in the course of probate your heirs and beneficiaries must be sent a copy of your will and a notice telling them when and where the will is to be probated. We've also seen that ordinarily two separate newspaper notices are run, for several weeks each, telling the general public that you've died, who your executor is, and when they can present claims to your estate.

Additionally, your will and all papers filed in probate court are *public records,* meaning anyone—yes, anyone—can get them, review them, and duplicate them at any time after your death until the end of time. Your will, your beneficiaries, those persons you have disinherited, your property (listed in the inventory), and any other business between your executor and the court—all this is available to anyone, at any time. This is how we all know what's in Howard Hughes's will (or wills): a newspaper reporter simply got into the court records, something any of us could have done.

It is these last three areas of probate—cost, delays, publicity—along with the complications and frustrations inherent in the process itself, that have caused many persons to want to avoid probate. Doing so is really quite simple, and the next chapter tells you how.

4

How to Avoid Probate

WE SAW in chapter 3 that there are three types of your property that definitely will escape probate when you die: proceeds on a life insurance policy (or on a retirement plan), unless they're payable to your estate; property that you held jointly with another who had a right of survivorship; and property that was held in a living trust that you established while you were alive. The purpose of this chapter is to explore in depth the last two of these three techniques for avoiding probate. As we shall see in this chapter and in the following chapters, a living trust is a far more beneficial estate-planning tool than is the creation of a joint tenancy, so we will review that method of avoiding probate first.

YOU CAN AVOID PROBATE BY ESTABLISHING A LIVING TRUST

Property in your living trust avoids probate when you die, and goes directly to the persons you named in the trust agreement. Because this can be very attractive to those who wish to avoid the hassles, publicity, cost, and delays of the probate process, let's take this subject step by step.

What is a trust? As we saw in chapter 2, a trust is simply an arrangement between you and another person (called the "trustee") whereby the trustee holds and manages some or all of your property, title to which you transfer over to him or her. The trustee is subject, of course, to your directions, and can do with your property only what you allow and direct him or her to do with it. At your death, the trustee distributes your property according to your instructions.

When can you establish a trust? There are two times at which a trust may be established. You can establish a testamentary trust under your will (discussed in chapter 2). Property held in a testamentary trust does not avoid probate; in fact, it must go through probate before it can pass to your testamentary trustee and before he can begin to administer and dispose of it. Obviously, a major problem with a testamentary trust is that since it arises under your will when you die, you cannot change it if you're dissatisfied with how it, or your trustee, is operating and paying off beneficiaries.

You can also establish a trust while you are alive. To establish a "living trust," you simply transfer some property to a trustee while you are alive, giving him instructions regarding its management and disposition both while you are alive and then after your death. Property held in a living trust does not go through probate when you die. When you establish the living trust, you can retain the right to amend or revoke the trust at any time up to your death.

What are the advantages of a trust? First, let's review briefly the advantages available through either a testamentary or living trust that were covered more fully in chapter 2. You can name the time your beneficiary is to receive your property; you can provide for competent management of your property; a trust can keep property in your family; a trust can put certain restrictions on property; a trust can give your family significant tax savings not otherwise available. At this time you may want to review the pages in chapter 2 in which these advantages of a trust were discussed.

What are the advantages of a living trust? Suppose you want the advantages that a trust can provide, but don't know whether a testamentary trust or a living trust is best for you. What advantages does a living trust have over a testamentary trust?

1. Property held in a living trust avoids probate at your death. This is so because once you transfer the property to the trustee, you are no longer its legal owner; the trustee is the owner. So at your death there is no need for the title-clearing functions of probate, which we discussed in chapter 3. Even the death of the trustee will have no effect on the property in trust, since a successor trustee will then take over. You yourself can name a successor trustee in the trust agreement ("If Joe Blow, the present trustee, for any reason becomes unable to continue as trustee, then Mary Blow shall act as successor trustee"), or if you have not named a succes-

sor trustee in your agreement or if the named successor trustee cannot perform the job, then the court can name a successor trustee. In any case, neither your death nor the death of a trustee makes probate necessary.

A living trust avoids the publicity, expense, and delays of probate that a testamentary trust would face. Let's look a little closer at each of these areas. First, a living trust avoids the publicity of probate. Remember that once a will is presented for probate in the probate court, it is from that time forevermore a public document, available to any person who pulls it out of the court records. Also remember that the inventory that your executor has to file is a public document too, and that it lists, for all persons to see, just exactly what property you owned when you died. In addition, there are the newspaper notices of the probate action. That's more publicity for you and your estate.

Because a living trust avoids probate, it avoids the publicity problems indicated above. When you die, the trust agreement is not sent to any of your heirs, it is not filed in court, no newspaper notice is published, no inventory of its contents is filed in court, and it is not available to the public or to the newspapers. The fact that you have a trust, the property in the trust, and the provisions of the trust are absolutely secret and confidential between you and your trustee.

A living trust also avoids the probate fees that average 5 percent of your probate estate. If you die with $100,000 worth of stock in your name alone, then it's going to cost $5,000 to get that stock probated. On the other hand, if you put it into a trust while you are alive, you would have saved the $5,000 in probate costs. But remember that unless you act as your own trustee, or a good friend undertakes this responsibility for you, you'll have to pay your trustee. You could possibly negotiate the fee for an individual trustee, and to some extent you can negotiate the fee payable to a corporate trustee. Corporate trust companies may have a minimum annual fee. It's wise to shop around.

A living trust also avoids the delays of probate. You may recall that in chapter 3 we saw there was *at least* a nine-month delay between the time you died and the time the property was distributed to your beneficiaries at the end of probate. For example, even if you simply leave everything you have to your spouse, it will still be at least nine months after your death before your spouse gets your property. True enough, in the meantime your spouse can collect the homestead, exempt property, and family allowances, but this may be a very small amount compared with the bulk of your estate, which will not go to your surviving spouse until the delays of probate are over. With a living trust, on the other hand, there are no delays, and after you die your trustee can distribute the trust property directly to your surviving spouse. Of course, whether your property is probated or is held in a living trust, your creditors and taxes have to be paid. But with a living trust, there's no additional delay in getting the balance of the property to your beneficiaries.

2. Another advantage of a living over a testamentary trust is that with a living trust you can see how well your chosen trustee performs his duties. Suppose you've decided upon a trust to hold your property for your beneficiaries after you die. You could simply set up a testamentary trust, and then hope that when your property is turned over to the trustee (at the end of your probate), he will do as you would have wanted. Under a testamentary trust arrangement, neither you nor your trustee will have an opportunity to see whether the trust will work to the satisfaction of both of you. Instead, you could set up a living trust, give your chosen trustee some money or some property right now, and let him try his hand

at managing it. You then would have the opportunity, while you are alive, to review your trustee's performance, and if you are dissatisfied, you can revoke the trust, or change it to give your trustee either more or less powers, or you can appoint another trustee.

3. A living trust can remove management responsibilities from your shoulders. Suppose you own a condominium apartment that you rent out or, say, you own some stocks. Managing a condominium apartment or playing the stock market day in and day out can get to be a very tedious business. But if you placed your condominium apartment or your stocks, or both, into a living trust, then it becomes the responsibility of your trustee to ensure that those assets are both safeguarded and kept productive. Your instructions will guide him. For example, if you want him to trade in stock only in companies located below the Mason-Dixon line, then tell him so. On the other hand, if you trust his judgment enough to let him have free rein with the stocks, then you can give him that free rein. The point is that he will manage your property in accordance with your directions. And while you're alive, you can change those directions at any time you want, as long as you made your trust "amendable" at the time of its establishment.

4. A fourth advantage a living trust has over a testamentary trust is that a living trust is less subject to attack by disappointed heirs than is a will. There are two common situations that seem to breed will attacks and will contests. These are: (1) the divided family, where there are children from a first marriage and a spouse and/or children from a second marriage; and (2) the "unnatural" disposition, where a spouse or child or other beneficiary gets either disproportionately more or less than his or her "natural" share. If you are in either of these situations, your will is in a "high risk"

area, and you should be aware that a disappointed heir could attack your will. Of course, to state the obvious, the mere fact that somebody is disappointed and brings a will contest doesn't mean necessarily that your will is going to be thrown out and that you will be declared intestate: the contestant has to win his contest. It does mean, however, that your executor is going to have to defend your will in court, and that means he has to hire an attorney, and it's going to take a lot of time and money to get this situation resolved. Whatever money it takes to defend your will will be paid out of your estate, of course, which means that your beneficiaries get less than they would if there had been no attack at all.

A living trust is much less subject to a successful attack than is a will. There are few cases in which a living trust has been declared invalid by the court. If you believe that there is a strong chance that someone will contest your will, then you and your attorney should investigate the possibility of a living trust. As we will shortly see, a living trust can dispose of your property when you die just as a will disposes of your property when you die, and since it offers the bonus of avoiding probate too, why not set up the trust?

5. A fifth advantage of a living over a testamentary trust is that a living trust avoids the problems of a guardianship if you become incompetent. Without a trust, if you became incompetent and unable to manage your property, the probate court would have to appoint somebody, called the guardian of your property, to manage your property for you. This court appointment would take time and cost money (to hire the lawyer to represent you), and there would be publicity. The guardian may have to post bond—payable out of your money. Furthermore, the guardian would have to submit his accountings to the court (usually annually), and this would take more time and money. On the other hand, the

trustee of your living trust can continue to manage your property despite your incompetence. If you're your own trustee, you would provide, in your trust, for a successor trustee to step in automatically upon your becoming incompetent. Your trustee would be authorized to make payments of principal and income to you and/or your family that are necessary for your and their living expenses, health, and comfort during your incompetency.

A living trust, therefore, has five major advantages over a testamentary trust: (1) it avoids probate; (2) it gives you a chance to see your trust and trustee in action, and to make changes if necessary; (3) it places the burden of managing your assets upon your trustee; (4) it is less subject to attack than is a will; and (5) in the event that you become incompetent, it provides for the management of your property without court involvement or interference. Let's see now what property you can put in a living trust.

What property can be placed into a trust? The answer to this is simple: anything from a birdcage to a battleship. A chair, a lamp, a piano, a house, a condominium, stocks, cash, a savings or checking account, bonds, an airplane—anything a person can own can be placed into trust.

Obviously, the type of asset you wish to transfer into trust will determine how the transfer to the trustee is recorded. If you transfer land or real property into trust, then a deed is the appropriate method of recording that transfer. If you want to transfer stock into trust, then on the reverse side of your stock certificate you simply transfer the shares over to "Joe Jones, Trustee," and then send the stock certificate back to the corporation to have the new owner recorded on the books of the corporation and a new certificate issued in the trustee's name. Personal property to which there is no recorded title—such as a chair or a piano—can be placed into trust by a simple execution of a "bill of sale," which is a paper whereby you acknowledge that you are assigning the property to the trustee. There are other ways of recording the transfer of other types of property, and your lawyer can certainly assist you with them.

What provisions can be made for the disposition of property and income held in a living trust? There are two time periods that are applicable with a living trust: while you are alive and after you are dead. For either time period, you can provide whatever you like with respect to distribution of income and principal from the trust. While you are alive you can have it paid directly to you, to your spouse, to your children, or to whomever you wish and in whatever shares you wish and at whatever time you wish.

What happens to the property in your trust after you die? This is where a living trust can act as a "will substitute." That is, you can put whatever provisions you would have put in your will right into your trust. You can disinherit. You can order the trust to end at your death and distribute all the assets immediately to your spouse or to your children in whatever shares you wish. Or if you want, you can continue the trust in either a simple or a sophisticated manner. Let's take two examples of this. In the example in chapter 2, Mary and Pete Miller provided for their ne'er-do-well son, George, and their unbusinesslike daughter, Jane, in their testamentary trusts. They could have made exactly the same provisions in living trusts.

Another way to continue your trust would simply be to provide that the trustee shall continue to manage the trust property for the benefit of your spouse and children, paying them whatever amounts of principal and income your spouse directs. The trust would end when your spouse has died and when your youngest child reaches, say, twenty-seven years of age. After your spouse has died and before your youngest child reaches twenty-seven, the trustee would make whatever distributions to your children as the trustee, in his or her discretion, felt to be necessary for whatever of the following purposes you choose: welfare, education, health, maintenance, support, comfort, travel, and so on. You pick the guidelines; the trustee carries them out. This type of trust, by the way, is called a "sprinkle trust" because your trustee has the discretion to sprinkle income and principal among your children when, if, and in the amounts they need it. This type of trust is extremely flexible, and therefore more frequently used than a flat direction to give each child X dollars. Life being what it is, some children will doubtless need, and deserve, more than others.

Who can be the trustee of your living trust? Any adult person and any trust company can act as your trustee. You should determine, on your own, whether the investment and management services that a professional corporation can give you are worth the fees that they will charge.

You can also appoint yourself as your own trustee. Naming yourself as trustee is the ideal way to have the many benefits of a living trust and yet retain the management of your property. In this case, the law considers that you are now two separate legal individuals, that is, you as an individual and you as a trustee. You as a trustee must act in accordance with the written directions given to you as trustee in the trust document by you as an individual.

Of course, if you name an individual, who could be yourself, as trustee, you will want to name a successor trustee to take over in the event your individual trustee cannot act as trustee any longer, for whatever reason (such as mental incompetence, disability, death, or just plain not wanting to do the job anymore). If your trust is to continue after you are dead (until, for example, your spouse has died and your youngest child has reached a certain age), then you will want to name several successor trustees, each to take over in the order that you have set. It is, of course, entirely possible, and in fact frequently done, for you to "backstop" all of your individual trustees with a corporate trustee. That way, if all the individual trustees fail to act for any reason, then the corporate trustee at least will always be there.

The duties of a trustee—custody and safeguarding of assets, record keeping, filing tax returns, preserving the trust principal and making it productive, and exercising impartial discretion to determine whether or not a beneficiary should be paid under the trust's provisions that you have established —can be split between two or more trustees. You could, for example, have a corporate trustee take care of the custodianship, record keeping, and tax-return responsibilities, while another trustee—perhaps you, your spouse, or a good friend or relative—could have the controlling voice with respect to investments and making distributions to your beneficiaries.

What records and tax returns need to be kept and filed? As we saw in the paragraphs immediately above, the creation of a trust creates a new legal entity, the trustee. You can think of the trustee as just another human being. Since that human being is probably going to have income coming to him from the trust's investments and disbursements going out to beneficiaries, it is clear that the trustee is going to have to keep clear records of income and disbursements. Because income is coming into the trust, income tax returns will have to be filed. Whether or not the trust pays an income tax depends on the type of trust you create. Also, just as human beings have Social Security numbers to identify themselves, your trust will have to apply for and use, in its tax reporting, a federal identification tax number to identify itself.

Should your living trust be irrevocable or revocable? An irrevocable living trust is one that, once it is made, cannot be revoked or amended by you in any way. A revocable living trust is one that can be both revoked by you and changed by you while you are alive. After your death it would become irrevocable unless you gave someone else the power to revoke or amend it. Either type of living trust will avoid probate. Either type of trust has the benefits that we have mentioned thus far. What, then, are the differences between an irrevocable and a revocable trust? Under an irrevocable trust you are giving up the opportunity to take the property back or to change the trust in any way, and so you are considered to be making a gift. A federal gift tax may be due (see chapter 5). Depending upon the provisions of the irrevocable trust, you may not be taxed on its income during your life and the trust property may not be subject at your death to the death tax. The problem with an irrevocable trust is obvious: it cannot be changed by you to meet changing circumstances or changing needs of beneficiaries. Because of the inflexible nature of this kind of trust, most people get into it only in order to avoid the income and death taxes (even though they have to pay the gift taxes).

On the other hand, the revocable living trust neither saves nor causes any taxes: it is, in terms of taxes, as if it had never been created. Since you can revoke the trust and take back the property at any time, the property is considered to be yours. You are therefore taxed on its income during your life and on its principal when you die. Just as there is no tax advantage in a revocable living trust, there is also no tax disadvantage. It is this kind of trust that most people prefer, as it may be changed at any time before their death.

What happens to your property when you die? When you die, your trustee will manage your trust property in accordance with your directions in the trust agreement. But what happens to all your other property? At death, your assets fall into two major subdivisions:

LSTC Property	Property in Your Name Alone or as Tenant in Common

   The left-hand box, you will remember, represents Life insurance, Survivorship property, property held in a living Trust, and your spouse's one half of the Community property.

   The disposition of property in your name alone or held as tenant in common with others is controlled under your will or, if you have none, under the intestacy laws. What this means is that even though you have a living trust, you still need a will to dispose of the property that you did not put into the trust. Of course, if you put every speck of property that you own into your trust, then your will simply would not cover any property when you die. But most people don't put all they own into the trust, and commonly their home, clothes, some jewelry, furniture, favorite dog, and so on, are left out.

   Many persons who have established a living trust write a very simple will, called a "pour-over will." Under this type of will you give your tangible personal property (car, furniture, clothing, etc.) to your spouse or children; then whatever property remains outside the trust is "poured over" into your living trust. Both the tangible personal property and the property destined for your trust go, of course, through probate. After probate your executor distributes the respective properties directly to your spouse and to the trustee of your living trust. The trustee then administers his property in accordance with your instructions in the trust agreement. This combination of a living trust and a pour-over will provides a "unified" estate plan.

To further integrate and centralize your estate plan, you can make your trust the beneficiary of your life insurance proceeds. Then, when you die, your life insurance companies will pay directly to the trust, and the trustee will be able to centrally manage and control the disposition of your assets —all in accordance with your instructions in the trust agreement. This orderly approach is often far preferable to the helter-skelter way many people "plan" for the distribution of their insurance proceeds. As life insurance proceeds comprise the largest single asset for most families (your family, too, probably), consider these further points on the advisability of putting insurance proceeds into a trust. (1) By placing insurance proceeds in your trust you can take steps to ensure the wise management of those funds. It is significant that insurance-company statistics show that 70 percent of all lump-sum payoffs are completely gone one year after the insured's death. There are probably many reasons for this: poor management, vulnerability of the beneficiary to poor investment schemes, "loans" to family members that are never intended to be repaid, and outright frauds. (2) Since a primary use of insurance proceeds is to provide ready cash at your death for debts, taxes, probate, and living expenses, thereby avoiding forced sales of your assets, you can guarantee those payments by paying the proceeds to a trustee rather than to a spouse or child, who may choose to visit the casinos of Las Vegas with the insurance money. (3) Do you want your children to inherit your insurance money when they reach legal age? Will they have the maturity and judgment to make the best use of the money? Wouldn't it be better to put it in a trust where it can be paid out for their needs as they arise, with the bulk of the money passing to the children when they are older?

It is possible to make your life insurance payable to a living trust. Or if you don't have or don't want a living trust but would like a trust arrangement to protect your insurance proceeds after your death, then you can set up a "life insurance trust" while you're alive. All this is, is a living trust that holds no property during your life, but you make your insurance proceeds payable to it. Then at your death the life insurance proceeds flow into trust, and your trustee goes to work in accordance with your directions. With a life insurance trust, usually no fees are payable to the trustee until you die and his work actually begins. And because the insurance money is paid to your trust and not to your estate, it is not subject to probate.

Let's put all of this together now and see how a trust document will carry out the objectives that John Thomas has decided upon for his estate. John has 500 shares of ABC stock in his name alone. He wants to avoid probate on his stock when he dies; to achieve this he decides to place the stock in a living trust. He wants the right to revoke or change the trust during his life, so he makes it revocable, and he wants to continue to manage the stock, so he makes himself the trustee. After he dies, he wants the income from the stocks and the stocks themselves to stay in trust, and to be paid out at the trustee's discretion to his wife and children until such time as his wife is dead and his youngest child is twenty-nine. At the time that both those events have occurred, he wants one half of the principal to be distributed equally among the children, and the other half to remain in trust for the children until the youngest is thirty-three, when it will be paid out to the children equally and the trust will end.

Here's a "translation," in simple English, of the revocable living trust John's attorney prepared for him. Again, this is not a form, and should not be used or copied by you. It is missing many of the technical legalities that would make it into a true trust.

THE JOHN THOMAS REVOCABLE LIVING TRUST

This agreement is made this _____ day of _____ , 19 _____ , by and between JOHN THOMAS of Chicago, Illinois, and JOHN THOMAS of Chicago, Illinois, as trustee.

The trustee acknowledges receipt of 500 shares of ABC stock, which will form the original principal of the trust. Anyone can add other property to the trust, with the permission of the trustee. JOHN THOMAS (called "John" for the rest of this document) retains the right to amend or revoke this trust at any time while he is alive; any revocation will also include directions to the trustee regarding what to do with the income and principal of the trust.

While John is alive, the trustee will pay him all the income of the trust, at least semiannually. The trustee will pay John, or any other person, principal only upon John's direction. If John becomes incompetent or for any other reason ceases to act as trustee, then the successor trustee (named below) will pay to John, his wife, and his children whatever amounts of income and principal are necessary for their health, maintenance, comfort, support, and education.

When John dies, the following instructions apply. The successor trustee will make payments of income and/or principal to John's wife and his children in whatever amounts, and as frequently as required, as the trustee shall think necessary or helpful for their health, education, maintenance, and support. The trustee is not required to make any payments, nor to keep payments equal or prorated; his discretion is controlling. The trustee will consider John's wife the preferred beneficiary of this trust, and will resolve uncertainties regarding distributions in her favor.

One half the trust principal will be distributed out of trust in equal shares to John's children when John's wife has died and the youngest living child reaches twenty-nine years of age. The remainder of the principal will be kept in trust, under the conditions noted in the paragraph just above, until John's wife has died and the youngest living child has reached thirty-three years of age, when it will be distributed in equal shares to his children then alive, and the trust will end. If, at either distribution, a child has died but left descendants, the descendants will take that child's equal share, per stirpes.

The trustees are as follows. John is the initial trustee. At his incompetence, death, or resignation, his brother, Gordon Thomas, will become successor trustee. At the incompetence, death, or resignation of Gordon as trustee, John's sister, Shirley Jones, will become trustee. At her death, incompetence, or resignation, then _____ Trust Company will become successor trustee.

The trustee can sell, exchange, or transfer the principal as he sees fit. He can buy whatever asset he thinks is wise. He can mortgage or lease the property. [*The trustee's powers are usually quite lengthy; you've probably got the idea, so we'll stop here.*]

This agreement has been signed by the parties and notarized on the date that appears on the first page.

s/John Thomas _____

s/John Thomas, Trustee _____

After setting up the trust, John discovers that he is very happy with the way the trust disposes of his ABC stock, and decides he would like all his property to go the same way at his death. He does this by having his attorney draft a pour-over will for him and by changing the beneficiary of his life insurance policy to "The John Thomas Revocable Living Trust Dated _____." Now John has an integrated and centralized estate plan.

How much does it cost to have an attorney draft a living trust? If you're going to set up a trust, you should do it right. Doing it right involves talking with your attorney to be sure you fully understand everything mentioned in this chapter. It also means setting up your trust in such a way that after you die it gives your estate the maximum tax advantages consistent with your wishes (see chapter 5). These areas of planning take time, but as we've seen in this chapter and will see in the next chapter, a little time and planning now can save a lot of money later on. I mention the time involved because generally attorneys charge on the basis of the time they spend. The time spent can vary greatly from client to client, since no two persons have the same estates, problems, or objectives. Putting all these variables together, it would probably be reasonable for you to expect to pay an attorney at least $400 to prepare a living trust for you. The best way to find out what it will cost you, of course, is simply to ask your attorney.

There are do-it-yourself form books available for the drafting of trust agreements, but I would caution you about using these on your own. The warnings mentioned earlier with regard to homemade wills apply equally here. It's very possible that you (or your heirs or beneficiaries) will spend more

money getting *out* of the problems created by your homemade trust than you would have paid an attorney in the first
place.

YOU CAN AVOID PROBATE BY JOINT TENANCY

The second way of avoiding probate is by having property
placed in joint tenancy or, as it's called if the property is held
by husband and wife, tenancy by the entirety. The advantages of joint tenancy, or tenancy by the entirety, are that it
is quite simple to arrange, and that, at the death of all joint
tenants except the last one, title immediately passes to the
remaining, alive, joint tenants without the delay, expense, or
legal entanglements and confusion of probate. (The survivors
will have to record the death of the deceased at the place
where title is held, but that's a lot quicker and easier than
probate.)

You may be paying a high price by having your property
in joint tenancy, however. First, remember that joint tenancy
or tenancy by the entirety does not avoid probate on the
death of the last owner. For example, if you and your wife
own your house as tenants by the entirety, and you and your
son have a joint checking account, then when you die, the
house will go to your wife and the account will go to your
son, both without probate. However, when your wife and
your son die later on, unless they have placed the house or
account in joint tenancy with others, the properties will have
to be probated because there are no more surviving joint
tenants. If the house or account was in a living trust, however, you could arrange it so that there would be no probate
at your death, the death of your wife, or the death of your
son.

A second disadvantage is that the jointly held property can easily end up in the hands of beneficiaries whom you did not intend to have it. For example, take the house that went to your wife. Suppose she remarries and, wanting to avoid probate at her death, makes her new husband a joint tenant in the ownership of the house. She then dies. Her new husband gets the whole house, and your children receive nothing, which is not what either of you intended. Or suppose she didn't change the ownership of the house, leaving it in her name alone. When she dies, her new husband will get a share of the house whether she died intestate (see the first diagram on page 7) or with a will (see chapter 2). Contrast this with the fact that he would have gotten *nothing* if the house had been held in a trust that named her and your children as beneficiaries.

Finally, change the example and assume that one spouse of a childless couple dies. All the jointly held property goes to the surviving spouse, and then when he or she dies without a will, the property goes according to that person's intestacy line—in other words, all to that spouse's relatives, thereby cutting out the relatives of the spouse who died first.

A third problem with joint tenancy is that a joint tenant's will does not control the property at all. If it is your intent to leave everything to your wife but you have joint checking and savings accounts with your son and daughter, respectively, then when you die they are going to get the checking and savings accounts, and your wife will not. If your children then try to give the accounts to your wife, they will be making a taxable gift on which they will have to pay a federal gift tax. That certainly is a mess that you hadn't contemplated.

The fourth problem with joint tenancy is that when it is created, it may also create a federal gift tax liability. If you

take $100,000 of your own stock and put it in joint tenancy
with your son, then you are obviously making him a gift. As
we'll see in the next chapter, any time you make a gift of
more than $10,000 per year to any one person, then you have
a possible gift tax liability. There are only two exceptions to
this gift tax rule on the creation of a joint tenancy. First, if
you and your spouse purchase real property as joint tenants
or as tenants by the entirety, then even though you put down
all of the money, the federal government allows you to defer
the tax consequences until either of you dies. This can be
both good and bad, as we'll see in the next chapter. Second,
on the creation of a joint checking or savings account with
any person, even though you put in all the money, no gift is
made until the other person, the nondepositor, withdraws
some of the money. At that point, clearly you are making a
gift to the other person.

Finally, in terms of death taxes, joint tenancy or tenancy
by the entirety is a very expensive way of holding property.
Many people mistakenly think that property held in joint
tenancy is not taxed when a joint tenant dies. This is not true.
In fact, holding property in joint tenancy can result in paying
a lot more death taxes than would be the case if the property
was held in a tenancy in common or as the separate property
of one of the parties. We'll see in chapter 5 that a very
frequently used estate-planning tool to save taxes is to take
property *out* of joint tenancy and to place it either into
tenancy in common or into the separate ownership of one
party alone.

5

The Federal Estate Tax and How to Reduce It

THE GOOD NEWS is that there are two separate exemptions, or deductions, from the federal estate tax: one exemption for property you leave your spouse, and a separate exemption for property you leave to any other person or persons. Any property you leave your spouse at your death is entirely tax-free, and there is no dollar limit. You can leave your spouse as much as you like, without tax.

If you leave property to any person or persons *other than* your spouse, then the exemption differs, depending upon the year in which you die.

YEAR OF YOUR DEATH	AMOUNT YOU CAN LEAVE TAX-FREE TO PERSONS OTHER THAN YOUR SPOUSE
1982	$225,000
1983	$275,000
1984	$325,000
1985	$400,000
1986	$500,000
1987 and thereafter	$600,000

Note that the exemption in any year ($400,000 in 1985, for example) is not an exemption per recipient; instead, it's a deduction from the sum total of your "estate," no matter how many or few persons you leave it to.

Example: Mary Lee dies in 1986. Her total "estate" is valued at $625,000. She leaves it all to her three children. Her federal exemption is $500,000. Her executor will pay a federal estate tax on the balance of $125,000. That federal tax is about $50,000, and it comes from Mary's estate; the balance of her estate, $575,000, goes to her three children.

Two warnings before we move ahead. First, the federal tax is on your "estate," and that word includes all property in your name alone, your interest as a tenant in common, *and* can even include the LSTC property—your Life insurance and retirement funds, your Survivorship property, your living Trust, and *your* half (not your spouse's half) of the Community property. Second, don't let the fact that you can leave your spouse limitless wealth without tax lull you and your family into a false sense of security. Later on, when your spouse dies and everything goes to the children, there is a definite dollar limitation to the amount they can get tax-free.

Example: You die in 1983 and leave your "estate" of $350,000 to your wife. No federal tax is due because it all went to your spouse. If your wife already has her own "estate" of $385,000, the sudden addition of your "estate" to hers increases her "estate" to $735,000, which is above the amount she can leave tax-free to the children. If she dies in 1987 or later, when her exemption is $600,-000, her executor would pay tax on $135,000. The federal tax on that amount is about $54,000. (But all is not lost—the balance of this chapter will show you how to get $1.2 *million* down to the kids, tax-free, if a little planning is done.)

At this point, you may be thinking, "Okay, I can leave my spouse anything I want tax-free, and she can leave the kids (or anyone else) up to $600,000 if she dies in 1987 or later. We don't need tax planning: my property and hers together won't even come close to $600,000." Well, if you're right about the value of your property and when you'll die, then you're right about not needing any help in avoiding federal taxes. You can skip the rest of this chapter. But before you do, consider these points: Are you sure you and your spouse will die in 1987 or later? If you die earlier, the exemption for property passing to the children (or anyone other than your spouse) will be less than $600,000. Also, if inflation continues, some of your estate may inflate (as well as appreciate), so that by 1987 your and your spouse's "estates" will in fact total over $600,000. Finally, let's have a close look at what the federal law taxes. As noted earlier, the federal tax is on your "estate," and your "estate" includes every asset, *every* bit of wealth, your name is on. You may have an "estate" worth a lot more than you think.

Let's take an example at this point that will show you two things: what's in your "estate," and how the federal estate tax works.

Suppose Husband has a valid will that says, "Everything goes to Wife." Husband dies in 1985. What does his estate pay in federal taxes? (Note: Any tax is deducted from Hus-

band's property before the property goes to Wife.) Here's
how to compute his tax:

A. *Add all assets.* (In each instance, put down date-of-death fair
market value of the asset, and not its original cost.)

 1. All separate property held in deceased's name alone (which
includes cash; debts or mortgages payable to him; personal property, such as jewelry, cars, furniture, clothes, planes, boats, race
horses, etc.; real estate here and abroad; stocks; bonds).

   Husband had: $ 110,000

 2. All deceased's interest in property held as a tenant in common
with another person or persons.

                     $ -0-

 3. Face values of all life insurance on deceased's life in which
deceased has a right (for example, the right to change the beneficiary, or to borrow against the policy, or to transfer the policy), or
which is payable to deceased's estate.

                 $ 65,000

   whole life policy on his life payable to Husband's estate,
and

                 $ 60,000

   group term policy on his life supplied by Husband's employer (Wife is beneficiary)

 4. All property held in deceased's revocable living trust.

                 $ -0-

 5. All property held in joint tenancy or tenancy by the entirety.

                 $ 15,000

   checking account with Wife;

                 $ 3,000

   savings account with Wife;

                $ 200,000

   home with Wife as tenants by the entirety

 6. Pension or profit-sharing proceeds.

                 $ 28,000

   from profit-sharing plan with employer (paid to Wife)

7. Partnership interest.

$ -0-

TOTAL HUSBAND'S ASSETS ("gross estate")

$ 481,000

B. *Subtract all liabilities.*
  1. Debts (Sears, Union Oil, etc.).
     Husband had: $ 6,000
  2. Mortgages and liens (on home, for example).

$ 109,000

  3. Funeral expenses.

$ 7,000

  4. Probate (5 percent of all separate property, or tenant-in-common property, including the proceeds of the life insurance policy paid to Husband's estate).

$ 9,000

  5. Casualty losses to deceased's property during probate.

$ -0-

TOTAL HUSBAND'S LIABILITIES

$ 131,000

The difference between Husband's assets and liabilities, $350,000, is his "net estate."

C. *Subtract any property left by deceased to charity.*

$ -0-

D. *Subtract the value of any property that goes to deceased's spouse.*
  Since Husband's will gave everything to Wife, subtract $350,000 from Net Estate of $350,000.

Net: $ -0-

E. *Subtract federal tax exemption for year of deceased's death.*

Net: $ -0-

F. *Take 40 percent of what remains.*

$ -0-

In paragraph F, when you take 40 percent of what remains, that 40 percent is, very roughly, the federal estate tax that the estate of the deceased owes. In our example above, at Husband's death, there is no federal estate tax to be paid. Before we move on to see what Wife will have to pay in estate taxes when she dies, let's look back for just half a second at paragraph D. The deduction taken there is known as the "marital deduction," because it allows the dying spouse to deduct from his estate any amount of property that is going to the surviving spouse. In our example Wife got everything that Husband had, either because he held it as a joint tenant or tenant by the entirety with Wife or because she was the beneficiary under one of his life insurance policies, or because he left everything else to her under his will.

Now let's see what happens to Wife when she dies later on, in 1990. Her valid will, let's suppose, gives all the property she's got to her children.

A. *Add all her assets.* When Husband died, she got everything that was available to be given to her, that is, she got Husband's net estate of $350,000. Additionally, she had the following assets of her own:

1. Separate property held in her name alone $ 60,000
2. Her interest in property held as a tenant in common $ -0-
3. Face value of insurance on her life $ 35,000
     whole life policy payable to the children, and $ 45,000
     group term policy supplied by her employer, payable to the children
4. All property in her revocable living trust $ 240,000
     (Wife inherited stocks from her parents and, to avoid probate, put them into a living trust.)
5. Property held in joint tenancy $ -0-
6. Pension $ 35,000
     (from pension plan, payable to children)   _____

Total Wife's own separate assets	$	415,000
Add Husband's net estate, which went to Wife	$	350,000
TOTAL WIFE'S ASSETS:		
(this is her "gross estate")	$	765,000
B. *Subtract all her liabilities.*		
1. Debts.	$	4,000
2. Funeral expenses.	$	5,000
3. Probate	$	21,000
TOTAL WIFE'S LIABILITIES:	$	30,000
Wife's net estate.	$	735,000
C. *Subtract gifts to charities.*	$	-0-
	Net: $	735,000
D. *Subtract property going to spouse.*	$	-0-
	Net: $	735,000
E. *Subtract federal tax exemption of $600,000.*		
	Net: $	135,000
F. *Take 40 percent of what remains.*		
	Tax: $	54,000

The estate going to Children would be Wife's net estate of $735,000 less the taxes of $54,000, or $681,000. Actually, the children will receive even less than this, since there are still *state* death taxes that have to be paid. Those are covered in the next chapter.

If you study this example carefully, you will see that this family ended up paying a rather large sum in federal taxes for the privilege of dying. Now for one more piece of bad news before we get to the good news. If you look at subparagraph F above, where you take 40 percent of what remains and that 40 percent is your federal estate tax, the bad news is that in fact it could be more than 40 percent. Like the income tax, the federal estate tax has graduated rates. The more you have, the higher percentage tax rate you have to pay. Forty percent is the minimum amount that you will have to pay; the percentage rate goes from 40 percent up to 50 percent (for taxable estates—that is, the amount in paragraph E in the example—of $2.5 million or more, after 1984).

Since this is going to get a lot more complicated before it gets much easier, let's just assume two things for the rest of this discussion. First of all, assume that everybody who reads this is going to live until 1987 or beyond, so that the full $600,000 exemption (step E) will be applicable. Second, just to simplify the picture, let's assume that no matter how much remains after step E we'll simply take 40 percent of that amount, remembering all the while that in fact the taxes could be a good deal larger than indicated by the number we get at step F, depending on the size of the estate.

Well, what are some of the ways you can reduce federal estate taxes? There are a great number of ways that this can be accomplished; we'll discuss the most frequently used in the following pages. You should know at the outset, however, that the tax law is extremely finicky and precise, and in many cases if the most inconsequential act is done or not done, the whole plan and device can be invalidated. Consequently, before embarking on any of the following tax plans, you should first consult your tax adviser, CPA, or attorney. So, with that warning, let's see some of the ways you can take advantage of the federal tax laws.

YOU CAN REDUCE YOUR TAXES THROUGH CAREFUL USE OF THE MARITAL DEDUCTION

The "marital deduction" is a very frequently used device that allows you to subtract from your estate any property that goes unconditionally to your spouse. There is no limitation on the amount of the deduction. But *unless you do it care-*

fully, the taxes on the surviving spouse's death later on, when the property passes to the children or someone else, can be monumental. Let's take an example of how to properly use the marital deduction.

Let's take our same Husband, Wife and two children. Remember that Husband's net estate (after subtracting all his mortgages, liabilities, probate expenses, and debts) was $350,000, and Wife's own seperate estate was $385,000. Suppose Husband and Wife have reciprocal wills, each of which says, "All to my spouse, but if I die second, then down to the children in equal shares." We saw that the taxes would be zero when Husband dies first and all his property goes to his wife, but would be $54,000 when Wife dies later and the property goes to the children. That's not so good. Can anything be done to reduce the $54,000? As a matter of fact, it's entirely possible to reduce the total taxes after both deaths to *zero.* What we're going to do here is use a trust, and here's how it works.

Husband redrafts his will so that the first $600,000 of his property goes into a testamentary trust for the exclusive benefit of his Wife, and the balance of his estate (if any) goes directly to her. Here's how his will would dispose of his property:

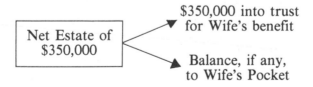

The idea here is that whatever amount, up to $600,000, that goes into the testamentary trust escapes tax *both* at Husband's death *and* at Wife's death, even though Wife gets advantages and benefits and use of it during her lifetime. By the use of this trust, we shelter up to $600,000 from the tax laws, and so the property passes from Husband to Wife and then down to the children, totally tax-free. This is how the taxation of Husband's and Wife's estates would now appear with Husband's new will:

Husband dies first. Husband has $350,000 in his net estate. He puts the entire $350,000 into a testamentary trust. The $600,000 federal tax exemption we all get reduces that amount to zero. Thus, his estate pays no tax at all.

Wife dies later on. To repeat, the $350,000 that Husband put into the testamentary trust for the exclusive benefit of Wife is not taxed at her death. Therefore, she is taxed only on what she owned, which happened to be $385,000. But since she gets $600,000 of her estate totally tax-free, she pays no taxes. Therefore, the total tax due after both deaths is zero.

In community property states, here is how the above discussion applies: if the $350,000 was Husband's separate property, then the marital deduction and the trust work exactly as noted above. On the other hand, if the $350,000 was the community property of Husband and Wife, then when Husband dies, only one half of that property, or $175,-000, would be his—the other one half belongs to Wife under the community property laws. Thus, Husband takes his $175,000, and rather than give it directly to Wife (which will only build up her taxable estate, causing more tax when she dies later on), he puts it into trust for her. His tax is zero (he had only $175,000, and the amount of his exemption is $600,-000), and Wife's tax when she dies later is zero also (she had her one half of the community property, worth $175,000, and her separate property of $385,000, and her exemption of $600,000 wipes that out; she is not taxed on the $175,000 Husband left in trust for her).

The legal costs to draw the documents would probably be

about 1 percent ($540) of the previous tax figure, resulting in a 99 percent savings on the taxes.

At this point, most people want to know more about this kind of trust that can pass property totally tax-free. Just what benefits can the Wife get out of this trust? Well, the bottom line is that we cannot give the Wife full, 100 percent control over the assets of this trust. To give her full control would mean giving her full ownership of that property, and it would be taxed at her death, which is exactly what we want to avoid. But if we can't give her complete ownership of this property, we can give her something close to it. What are the maximum benefits we can give her and still avoid taxation at her death?

(1) We can give her all the income that the trust earns. If you figure a modest interest rate of 6 percent on the trust assets of $350,000, then that means that she'll be getting $21,000 per year of income out of the trust.

(2) We can give her as much of the principal in the trust (that is, of the $350,000 itself) as she needs, in the trustee's judgment, for her health, maintenance, support, travel, comfort, welfare, reasonable luxuries, education, and so on. This will ensure that she can continue with her accustomed standard of living. The trustee will review the wife's living standards and situation, and if he sees that she needs any of the principal for any of the above reasons, then he simply distributes it to her. Since the distribution of principal is going to be in the trustee's discretion, who should be the trustee of this testamentary trust? You want to pick someone with good business sense who is going to get along well with your wife. It may be your brother, your parents, your children, a close friend, or a trust company. Your wife may even be her

own trustee. If she is her own trustee, her rights to use the principal for herself must be limited only to "health, education, maintenance, and support." Inclusion of other rights (travel, comfort, welfare) will result in the loss of the tax exemption you are trying to achieve.

(3) We can give the wife, whether or not she is the trustee, the right to take out the principal for her health, education, maintenance, and support. She cannot take it out for any other purpose. If the trustee decides not to make any distribution to the wife under its authority to invade principal, the wife herself can step in and take out principal for those four purposes. You might note that the wife's right to take principal for these four purposes really allows her to use the principal for her normal living expenses. She needn't be a pauper.

(4) The fourth right the wife could have to the property held in the husband's testamentary trust is called a "5-or-5" power. If given to her by the husband, this power authorizes the wife, over and above all the rights she has thus far, to demand that the trustee distribute to her out of the trust, on an annual basis, the *greater* of $5,000 or 5 percent of the principal. So if she wants to go to Paris, this is her ticket. This right is noncumulative, so that if the wife does not use it in one year, the next year she would not have the right to demand withdrawal of the greater of $10,000 or 10 percent. If the wife does have this right, then in the year she dies the federal government will add into her taxable estate the greater of 5 percent of the principal or $5,000, whether she exercised the right that year or not, but it won't add in any more principal than that.

We can't give the wife any further rights to the husband's testamentary trust because, if we do, then when she dies later on, her estate will be taxed on the property that remains in trust. But if you review the rights the wife has to the testamentary trust, you will see that in fact they are extremely generous. She gets all the income, and she can withdraw the principal whenever she needs it. The trust gives her benefits, protection, and security. And, don't forget that the bottom line on all of this is that the $350,000 held in trust for the wife will not be taxed when she dies (except for the 5-or-5 amount) and will pass to the children totally tax-free. And, as an extra bonus, none of that $350,000 will be probated, because it's in a trust. Thus the children get it without paying probate fees of $17,500 (5 percent of $350,000). Another advantage is that because the $350,000 is in a trust, its distribution to the children can be delayed after the wife's death until they reach whatever age the husband sets in his will. And if he wanted to, he could give the wife the right to change that age or even change the amounts going to the children. This right can be very valuable because it enables the wife to take a "second look" at the children and how they're doing after the husband has passed on, and make any adjustments that are needed.

This kind of trust, which gives a spouse benefits but which bypasses taxation at her (or his) later death, is called a "bypass" trust. A bypass trust can be built into a living trust, or, as in our example above, it can be a testamentary bypass trust.

At this point our hypothetical Husband and Wife, very happy with the advantages of a bypass trust, go ahead and change Husband's will to use a bypass trust exactly like the one noted above. The result is that if Husband dies first, no taxes are paid at all, even after Wife's later death. Are Husband and Wife finished with their tax planning now? Not yet, because we have been assuming all along that Husband will die first. If we are wrong in this supposition and in fact Wife dies first, what happens then? Well, let's have a look:

1. Think of it this way: Wife has $385,000 in her estate; Husband has $350,000 in his estate. If Wife has a simple will, leaving everything to Husband, and she dies first, no federal taxes will be due because of her unlimited marital deduction. However, now Husband's estate is increased by Wife's $385,000, up to $735,000. When he dies, after his $600,000 exemption is subtracted, he'll have $135,000 to pay taxes on. At the 40 percent rate, the taxes are $54,000.

2. In short, Wife made the same mistake Husband made earlier: she simply left all her estate directly to him, boosting his augmented estate over his $600,000 exemption. She should *not* have left her estate to her husband. Instead, she should have left it in a bypass trust for him.

3. If Wife provides that her $385,000 estate goes to a bypass trust, rather than directly to Husband, then on her death there would be no tax because of her $600,000 exemption. Husband then gets the use of the bypass trust for his remaining lifetime, as explained above, but does *not* get taxed on it when he dies. Thus, at his death only his $350,000 estate is taxed, but his $600,000 exemption means that no tax is due.

The result is this: if Husband's estate and Wife's estate *together* total more than $600,000, each spouse should have a bypass trust to save the children taxes.

Using our rough system of estimating taxes, let's see approximately how much in taxes our Husband and Wife can save their two children by using bypass trusts. Again, we'll assume Husband has some property, Wife has some property, and that they want to know whether each should use a simple will (which gives all his or her property to the other spouse outright), or whether they should get professional tax-avoidance help that will center on the use of bypass trusts rather than simple wills. Some rough figures are given in the table on the opposite page. The figures in the table are, of

TAXES SAVED WITH BYPASS TRUSTS

H's + W's Total Net Estates, Added Together	Taxes the Children Pay After H + W Are Both Dead		Taxes Saved for the Children with Bypass Trust
	If No Bypass Trust Used	If Bypass Trust Used	
$ 600,000 or less	-0-	-0-	-0-
700,000	$ 40,000	-0-	$ 40,000
800,000	80,000	-0-	80,000
1,000,000	160,000	-0-	160,000
1,200,000	240,000	-0-	240,000
1,500,000	360,000	$120,000	240,000
2,000,000	560,000	320,000	240,000

course, only approximations, and do not include additional savings that Husband and Wife will realize with a bypass trust, since the property in the bypass trust won't go through probate at the death of the surviving spouse.

As you can see from the table, if Husband and Wife both use bypass trusts (with professional help), they can transfer up to $1.2 million, totally tax-free, down to their children (or to any other beneficiary) after they both die.

YOU CAN REDUCE YOUR TAXES BY MAKING GIFTS

This will be a surprise to many people, but not only are there federal income and estate taxes, but there is also a gift tax. If you make a gift to me, or to anyone else, it may be subject to a federal gift tax. The tables used to determine the amount of gift tax are exactly the same tables used to determine the amount of death tax. Therefore, you might wonder what advantage there is to giving property away while you are alive if, when you die, exactly the same tax table is used to figure out the tax payable on that property.

In fact there are two reasons for making lifetime gifts. The first is that you remove any appreciation on the asset from your estate. Example: you have a rental house with a present net worth of $50,000 that you know you want your daughter to have after you're gone. If you hold it until you die, it might very well be worth $150,000. The $100,000 that the house has appreciated between now and your death will cost your estate an extra $40,000 in taxes (figuring taxes at the 40 percent rate, and assuming your estate used up all your other exemptions). By giving your daughter the property now rather than holding it until your death, you can save that $40,000 in taxes.

The second reason for making lifetime gifts is that you get two separate special exemptions for gifts made during your life that you do not get if you pass the same property when you die. These exemptions are unique to lifetime gifts.

1. The first exemption is that while you are alive, you can make a gift of $10,000 every year to as many different people as you like (whether they're in your family or not) without having to pay any gift tax on those gifts at all. Therefore, you can give each of your five children $10,000 this year, for a total of $50,000, without paying any gift tax whatsoever. And you can do the same thing again next year and the following year, and so on, so that after, say, ten years of this gift program, you will have removed $500,000 from your estate. That's $500,000 you will have gotten down to the people you want to benefit, without having to pay any gift or death taxes whatsoever on the transfers. If, on the other hand, you had passed that $500,000 down to your children under your will, then we've already seen that that amount would have been included in your taxable estate at death. If you had $600,000 of other property after subtracting your marital deduction, then that $500,000 would be taxed at the 40 percent rate: $200,000 would be lost to taxes!

2. The second special exemption for lifetime gifts is that your spouse can join with you and authorize you to use her or his $10,000 exemption in gifts you are making to other people. Therefore, for example, rather than giving just $10,000 of your money to each of your five children, you can, with your spouse's permission, give $20,000 to each of your children every year, totally tax-free. Even though the $20,-000 is actually your money, if your spouse agrees, you can use her or his $10,000 exemption for each of your gifts. Therefore, you can give away a total of $100,000 to all of your five children every year, meaning that after ten years you will have reduced your taxable estate by $1 million.

3. A third exemption for lifetime gifts is for gifts from one spouse to the other. In addition to the $10,000 annual exemption noted above, one spouse can give the other spouse, over the course of the donor's lifetime, an unlimited amount of property totally tax-free.

How can we put this to work? Well, let's take a simple example. Suppose Husband has an estate of $1.2 million, and Wife has no estate of her own. *If he dies first,* he can leave Wife $600,000 as a marital deduction (no tax due) and leave the other $600,000 in a bypass trust for her (no tax due because of his $600,000 exemption). See the table on page 113. When Wife dies later on, she's not taxed on the bypass trust, so it can go to the kids tax-free, and is only taxed on the $600,000 Husband left her. Her own $600,000 exemption wipes that out, so that property too goes to the kids tax-free.

But what happens if *Wife* dies first? Then when Husband dies later on, he has no marital deduction (because he has no wife he's leaving anything to), and has only the $600,000 exemption. That leaves $600,000 exposed to taxation, and, at the 40 percent rate, that means $240,000 is paid in federal taxes. Here's how to reduce those taxes to zero.

Husband should consider giving Wife $600,000 of his property. There would be no gift tax, because he can give her (and vice versa) limitless wealth without a gift tax. Husband should then have a bypass trust for his $600,000, and Wife should have the identical plan. Then, no matter who dies first, there will be zero taxes: no tax when the deceased's property goes into the bypass trust (because of the $600,000 exemption), and no tax when the surviving spouse dies later on (again, the bypass trust is not taxed, and the $600,000 exemption wipes out the rest.)

Note that if after exhausting your gift tax exemptions (as explained above) you have a net gift on which you have to pay tax, you can use your $600,000 federal estate tax exemption to wipe out, or reduce, that remaining gift. The catch is, though, that if you use part or all of your $600,000 during your life, you get only the balance at your death. Nevertheless, people do use the $600,000 exemption so that they don't have to pay any gift tax right now out of their pockets. As an example, suppose you give $50,000 of your stocks to your daughter. If your spouse joins in, you can deduct $20,000 from the gift, so you pay gift taxes on only $30,000. The gift tax has to be paid out of your pocket, since the donor is responsible for the tax. To wipe out the $30,000, you could use $30,000 of your $600,000 exemption, leaving you with a reservoir of $570,000 for future gifts or against your death tax.

There are three warnings about gifts. First, in order to qualify as a "gift" that Uncle Sam will exclude from your taxable estate, the transaction must leave you, the donor, with absolutely no strings with which you can pull the gift back. The donor must separate himself or herself from all right, title, and ownership to the gifted property. Therefore, for example, if a father decides to give some stocks to his son but retains the right to receive the dividends, or if he gives his house to his daughter but retains the right to live there for the rest of his life, these will not be recognized as true gifts for federal tax purposes, and the stocks and the house will be included in the father's taxable estate when he dies. This brings us to the second warning, which is that before making a gift, you should be sure to get professional advice. In rare instances, the $10,000 annual exemption is not available. Other complications can also arise: for example, gifts to minors require special attention. The final warning is the most obvious: don't make a gift just to save the tax. If you are going to need the property sometime in the future, then don't give it away. Even though you might give it to your children expecting them to give it back to you if and when you should need it, there are many sad cases in which the children decided not to give the gift back. No family needs that kind of strain.

YOU CAN REDUCE YOUR TAXES BY GIVING AWAY YOUR LIFE INSURANCE

Many people think life insurance is not taxed. This, unfortunately, is not true. Take these three examples:

1. *Life insurance paid to your spouse is tax-free.* Since you can leave any amount of wealth to your spouse tax-free at your death, you can leave her or him any amount of life insurance tax-free also. But while there is no tax at *your* death, at your spouse's later death your life insurance money makes up part of her or his estate. If that estate is over the $600,000 limitation, there will be a tax before the estate goes to the children. This tax at the second spouse's death can be completely avoided with a trust, discussed later in this section.

2. *Life insurance paid to a charity is tax-free.* Any property, including life insurance, paid to a charity at your death escapes estate taxes.

3. *Life insurance paid to anyone else is potentially taxable.* If, at your death, life insurance on your life is paid to anyone except your spouse or a charity, it counts as part of your estate, and is subject to the $600,000 limitation. For example, suppose you had a $100,-000 policy on your life payable to your daughter, Ruth. Your "estate" would include that $100,000. If your estate was then over the $600,000 limit, it would pay an estate tax; if not, there would be no estate tax.

Example: Your spouse is decreased, and you leave all your property worth $550,000 to your daughter, Ruth. You also name her as beneficiary on your $100,000 life insurance policy. For taxation purposes, your "estate" is $650,000. After subtracting your exemption of $600,000, the estate tax is $20,000 (40 percent of $50,000).

In this third category, the technical rule is that the policy is added into your estate if (1) it's on your life, and (2) you "owned" the policy at your death.

"Owning" a life insurance policy means that you have any of the following rights: to change the beneficiary, to pledge the policy for a loan, to borrow against the cash surrender value of the policy, to give the policy away, to cancel the policy and get back the cash surrender value, and many others. (The usual acid test on "owning" a policy is whether or not you have the right to change the beneficiary: if you do, then you "own" the policy; if not, then you will not own the policy only if you have none of the other rights of ownership as listed above.)

Now, if someone else (for example, your wife or child) "owned" the policy on your life, then at your death they'd still get the proceeds (no change there), but the proceeds would *not* be included in your taxable estate. Therefore, one frequently used estate-planning device is to have an insured person give away the ownership of his or her life insurance policy. Most types of policies (such as whole life, term, and group term) can be transferred. For example, you could give your policy to your spouse. This is called "spouse-owned" life insurance. This tactic was very popular before 1982, but is not needed any longer, because whether you make your spouse the owner or the beneficiary, in either case the proceeds won't be taxed at your death. Additionally, "spouse-owned" insurance had a major problem: if you and your spouse divorced, she (or he) might walk off with your insurance coverage. In short, "spouse-owned" insurance probably won't be used much more.

However, if your insurance is payable to someone *other than* your spouse, you might consider transferring the policy to that beneficiary. For example, if you owned a $100,000 policy on your life payable to your daughter, Ruth, at your death you'd pay (assuming you had $600,000 of other property that did not qualify for a marital or charitable deduction) 40 percent of it, or $40,000, in taxes for the privilege of owning that policy. If, on the other hand, you gave that policy to Ruth more than three years before you died, then none of that $100,000 would be taxed and your estate would save that $40,000.

At this point you may be wondering where the gift tax comes into all of this. Since you made a gift of that policy to Ruth, how much do you have to pay in taxes for the gift? The gift tax is figured *not* on the face value of the policy but on its replacement value, which is determined as follows: if it's a whole life policy, its replacement value is just about its cash surrender value (which you can reduce by borrowing against the policy before gifting it to Ruth). If the policy is a term or a group term policy, then its replacement value is very little, most probably under the $10,000 you can give Ruth in any year. The point is that when you give away a life insurance policy, there will be very little, if any, gift tax due, even though you save your estate a substantial amount of tax when you die later on.

Let's take this discussion on insurance just a little bit further. Suppose Husband decides to give his policies to Wife, or retains ownership himself and names her as beneficiary. The proceeds are not taxed in his estate. So far, so good. But let's remember that when he dies, Wife gets the proceeds, so when she dies later on, those proceeds (unless they're spent) will be included and may be taxed in her estate. Therefore, he has avoided being taxed in one estate, only to get caught in another estate. How can we avoid taxes on those proceeds in *both* estates? This is really quite easy: rather than giving the policy to Wife, the insured Husband puts the policy into a living, irrevocable, bypass trust. The trust is structured so that Wife gets the same benefits of income, principal, and 5-or-5 rights that we saw in the bypass trust discussed earlier. When Husband dies, there is no tax in his estate caused by the policies, because he doesn't own them: the trust owns the policies. The proceeds are then paid into the trust; Wife gets the benefits of the proceeds for her life, and at her death the remainder of the proceeds flow down to the children totally tax-free. That's a very good arrangement, but it can get even better. Because the proceeds are in fact in a trust, Husband can say, if he wants, that when Wife dies the proceeds don't get paid to the children till the youngest reaches, say, thirty-five years of age; in the meantime the proceeds can be used for the children's education, health, maintenance, support—or in whatever way Husband specifies. This kind of life insurance trust, then, avoids taxation at Husband's death, gives Wife full benefits and protection during her life, avoids taxation at Wife's death, protects the children until they are at a responsible age, and then distributes to them, totally tax-free. It's not easy to do much better than that.

YOU CAN REDUCE YOUR TAXES BY AVOIDING PROPERTY HELD JOINTLY

A lot of property is held in joint tenancy with right of survivorship or in tenancy by the entirety. There is a very common misconception that this property will avoid taxes when one of the joint tenants dies. This is not exactly correct. It will avoid *probate* if there's at least one joint tenant alive, and it may or may not avoid *taxes*.

If you own property with your *spouse* as joint tenants with right of survivorship or as tenants by the entirety, then when one spouse dies, the surviving spouse gets the entire property. There is no probate (see chapter 4). Also, there is no federal tax, because one spouse can leave an unlimited amount of property to the other, tax-free.

However, if you and anyone *other than* your spouse own property as joint tenants with right of survivorship, then when one of you dies, there may very well be a federal tax. Let's take this example to see how the tax law works. Father and Daughter own a house as joint tenants with right of survivorship. Father dies. At his date of death the property is worth, net of the mortgage, $100,000. Unless Daughter can prove to the Internal Revenue Service that she contributed her own cash dollars to the purchase of the house—either by paying the down payment or by paying the mortgage—100 percent of the value will be taxed in Father's estate. If Daughter can prove, for example, that 30 percent of the value was contributed by her own dollars, then only 70 percent will be included in Father's estate.

Let's assume Daughter can prove that she contributed 30 percent toward the purchase of the house. The balance of $70,000 will therefore be included in Father's estate. Father has the $600,000 exemption to reduce or wipe out this $70,000. But if Father is wealthy and has already used up his $600,000 exemption, then this $70,000 will be fully taxed in his estate at the 40 percent rate.

Now we have to see what happens when Daughter dies later on. When Father died, Daughter received the entire house because she was the surviving joint tenant. When she dies later on, 100 percent of the value of the property will be taxed in her estate, at the value it has as of the date of her death, less any encumbrances or mortgages on the property at that time. In other words, the house got taxed twice: once at Father's death, and then again at Daughter's death.

To summarize: property held jointly with your spouse avoids probate and federal taxes when the *first* spouse dies; property held jointly with a nonspouse avoids probate but may not avoid federal taxes when the *first* owner dies. Those results may seem desirable, but don't be deluded: we have to look at what happens when the *surviving* owner dies later on. Remember that when the first owner died, the surviving owner received the entire property (that's the meaning and essence of joint tenancy or tenancy by the entirety). Thus, when the surviving owner dies later on, 100 percent of the value of the property will be subject to tax.

Take this very common example. Husband and Wife own $800,000 worth of property in both their names, as joint tenants with right of survivorship or as tenants by the entirety. Wife dies. Husband now owns all of that property in his name alone. There was no probate or federal tax due when Wife died. Now, however, Husband owns $200,000 worth of assets *more* than the $600,000 he can leave, tax-free, at his death. Unless he can give that $200,000 away in $10,000 yearly increments before his death, his beneficiaries will be paying a federal estate tax of 40 percent on anything over $600,000. Here's how Husband and Wife could have set up their wills to avoid *all* federal taxes.

Suppose Husband and Wife hold the following property as joint tenants: home (net value $250,000), cash ($150,000), stocks ($180,000), rental unit at a nearby resort (net value $150,000), and miscellaneous personal property (furniture, cars, so on: $70,000). Total net value: $800,000.

How do we avoid the taxes we know will be due when both spouses are dead? We divide all assets in half. The home and rental unit are redeeded to "tenants in common," half for Husband and half for Wife. The cash and stocks are put into separate accounts, half for Husband and half for Wife. Now Husband has assets of $400,000, and Wife has assets of $400,000. Each spouse writes a will that contains a bypass trust, which gives the surviving spouse full benefits and protection without causing any tax when the trust beneficiary dies. Now Wife dies. Her property of $400,000 is tax-free, because it is less than the $600,000 exemption. It remains in trust for Husband's use. Husband now dies. He's not taxed on Wife's trust, even though he had full benefits from it, and he's taxed only on his $400,000. Since that's below his $600,000 exemption, he pays no tax. Thus, all the property goes directly to the children, totally tax-free. We've saved them $80,000 in taxes.

There's one other warning that should be made about

jointly held property. Perhaps it can best be seen by an example. If Husband and Wife both have beautifully drawn wills, which use bypass trusts that we have been talking about and have all kinds of fancy tax-avoidance gimmicks and devices in them but hold all their property as joint tenants, then one of those wills is wasted. This is because when the first spouse dies, all of his or her property is going to go directly to the other as surviving joint tenant and does not pass under the will. The will never has a chance to put its devices to work. This kind of oversight occurs frequently, so remember to check on how your property is held.

YOU CAN REDUCE YOUR TAXES BY EQUALIZING HUSBAND'S ESTATE AND WIFE'S ESTATE

As we saw in the example just above, a good amount of estate taxes can be saved if Husband and Wife try to equalize their separate estates by holding their property in their separate names, or as tenants in common, and then use bypass trusts in their wills. In fact, for a long time the soundest estate-planning advice was "Equalize your estates and use bypass trusts," and that advice is still good today.

Of course, not every husband and wife need worry about equalizing estates. Depending on their exemptions (for example, the $600,000 exemption), they may be able to get away with one spouse owning all or most of the property, or with holding all or most of the property in joint tenancy. But nonequalization is dangerous, because even though the property may escape taxes if husband and wife died *today,* it's certain that inflation and appreciation will drive the values of their property up, so that when they die in the future, their property value may very well exceed all the exemptions, which means they'll end up paying an estate tax. It's a good idea, therefore, to plan for future inflation and appreciation by having Husband own as much, in his separate name, as Wife owns in her separate name.

It's relatively simple to equalize estates if both Husband and Wife work. All you need to do is avoid joint tenancy and tenancy by the entirety ownership arrangements. Husband should keep his earnings, inheritances, and property in his own name, and Wife should do the same for her earnings, inheritances, and property. Holding property as tenants in common is also okay. The main idea is that you want to avoid joint tenancy or tenancy by the entirety arrangements between the spouses. If you do put your property into joint tenancy or tenancy by the entirety, then, if you want to save estate taxes, it will just have to be divided later on. This is not to say, however, that no property should be held jointly or by the entirety with your spouse. Oftentimes the family home and a small checking or savings account are held jointly to provide the surviving spouse with absolute assurance that she or he will have 100 percent ownership and control over that property.

If only one spouse works, then the only way to equalize estates is for the working spouse to make gifts to the non-working spouse, or for the nonworking spouse to inherit property (unless, of course, they live in a community property state, where the law automatically splits the salary between the spouses). As we've seen, a gift from one spouse to another will not involve a gift tax, since one spouse can give unlimited assets to the other free of gift tax. Therefore you can give your "poorer" spouse anything you want without paying any gift tax at all, and this could equalize your estates.

A final word on equalization of estates. It should be done with professional guidance. Why? Because (1) not everyone

needs it; (2) not everyone wants the surviving spouse to have
to deal with the bypass trust that the first spouse sets up, even
if it will save taxes; (3) not all assets have to be held separately by Husband or Wife; some can and should be held
jointly or by the entirety; (4) the bypass trust has to be
drafted very carefully.

YOU CAN REDUCE THE ULTIMATE TAX PAYABLE WITH A GENERATION-SKIPPING TRUST

This is an extension of the bypass trust concept. Say you and
your spouse are grandparents. You have three children, and
a lot of grandchildren. If you leave your property to your
children without placing it in a trust, then it may be taxed
when you die (depending on whether your estate exceeds its
exemptions), and may be taxed again when they die, meaning
that your property could have been taxed twice before the
grandchildren get it. You can eliminate the tax at your children's level if, instead of leaving the property to them without placing it in a trust, you set up three bypass trusts, one
for each child. We've seen all the benefits the child can get
from his bypass trust: security, protection, all the income,
principal when needed, and 5-or-5 powers. Under this arrangement the trust would not be taxed at your child's death,
and could, in fact, continue on for his or her children's
benefit. Later, when his or her youngest child reached, say,
twenty-one, the trust would end and the property would be
given to those grandchildren. In this way you would have
skipped one tax, the one at your child's death.

Two points about these generation-skipping trusts. First,
these types of trusts were, and to some extent still are, extremely favored by the wealthy because they allow succeeding

generations to enjoy property without paying taxes on it. In its zeal for equal treatment of all of us, the Tax Reform Act of 1976 put some severe dents in these trusts. The law on them is now especially complicated, so get advice in this area from an expert. Second, one of the Reform Act's dents is that only the first $250,000 in the bypass trust for each child escapes tax at that child's death. But with three children, that's $750,000 you can "skip a tax" on, so the trusts can still be quite useful.

WHAT OTHER WAYS ARE THERE TO REDUCE YOUR TAXES?

There are many other ways to reduce your taxes: private annuities, installment sales, family corporations, family partnerships, charitable remainder annuity trusts—the list goes on. What we've talked about thus far in detail are those estate-planning, tax-savings devices that are commonly used by many, many people. There are a great number of other, more esoteric devices that, given the proper circumstances and the proper objectives, can certainly be used to effect a good tax savings. The point to be made is that each different person has different assets, a different family situation, different plans, different objectives. A proper estate plan is unique to each person. There is always a plan that is totally right for each person. Even though there may have to be trade-offs in order to accomplish all the objectives, some plan will be found that is exactly right for you.

One final word of caution. In order to make the foregoing discussion somewhat palatable, I've had to simplify a few points and smooth over some rough edges. The fundamental ideas, however, are as I have stated them. Before you go charging off into any particular "tax savings" device or scheme, you should get some professional advice. The tax laws change very frequently, and as I've stated before, in order to get the benefits that you want, you have to do it exactly right. Uncle Sam gets very disturbed unless you recite back to him chapter and verse. He doesn't really have much of a sense of humor.

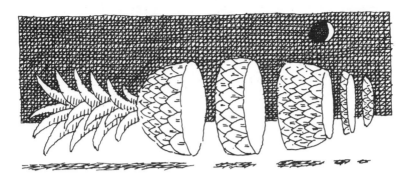

6

The State Inheritance Tax

AFTER THE numerous confusions of the federal estate tax, this discussion should be like a fresh breeze. Another piece of good news is that generally the state inheritance tax can be considerably less than the federal tax. Consequently, most people do not "plan" for the state inheritance tax and, instead, focus their attention on the federal tax.

The inheritance tax of most states is determined on a recipient-by-recipient basis. There is no lump-sum $600,000 exemption, as there is under the federal tax, but instead each specific beneficiary gets his or her own separate exemption. An example will show how this works.

John has the following nonprobate assets:

1. $25,000 life insurance policy payable to Son.

2. $25,000 life insurance policy payable to Daughter.

3. $50,000 life insurance policy payable to Wife.

4. House held as tenants by the entirety, present value $150,000, mortgage $30,000. Wife paid no cash toward the purchase of this house.

5. $10,000 checking account jointly held with Brother.

For his probate assets, John has a will that states:

1. My $55,000 worth of stocks goes to Son;

2. $10,000 of cash goes to Daughter;

3. My automobile goes to my Brother (John's car is worth $5,000);

4. The residue goes to my Wife (the residue of John's probate estate is $100,000).

The first step in determining John's state inheritance tax is to determine the net amount each recipient gets. In order to get the net value, first we have to figure the costs.

1. Probate costs (5 percent of probate assets of $170,000)	$ 8,500
2. Burial expenses	$ 2,500
3. Claims against estate	$ 3,000
4. Federal estate taxes	-o-
Total	$14,000

Assume all costs are paid out of the residue of the probate estate (as they normally are), so Wife gets $100,000 − $14,000 = $86,000.

Now, total the net amount each party gets.

	Wife	*Son*
	$ 86,000 (residue)	$55,000 (stocks)
	$ 50,000 (life ins.)	$25,000 (life ins.)
	$120,000 (house)	
Net Totals	$256,000	$80,000

	Daughter	*Brother*
	$ 10,000 (cash)	$ 5,000 (car)
	$ 25,000 (life ins.)	$ 10,000 (chkg. acct.)
Net Totals	$ 35,000	$ 15,000

After you determine the net amount each beneficiary gets, there may be specific exemptions that can be subtracted from each beneficiary's net amount. These exemptions vary from state to state, but a representative sampling might include:

1. On any joint tenancy going to a beneficiary: you can subtract any amount that the beneficiary can prove he or she contributed out of his or her pocket to the net value of the asset.

2. On a joint tenancy or tenancy by the entirety with your spouse: you can subtract a minimum of one half the net value of the property, and more if the surviving spouse can prove she or he contributed more than half to the net value of the property.

3. Life insurance proceeds: any life insurance proceeds payable directly to any beneficiary other than your estate can be subtracted. If the proceeds are paid to your estate, then they are not subtracted.

4. The first $30,000 of pension proceeds payable on your death to your spouse, children, parents, brothers, or sisters may be subtracted.

5. Any amounts paid to a charity may be subtracted.

Let's assume John's state authorizes all these exemptions. The next step is to subtract the exemptions (the applicable exemptions are the life insurance, one half of all tenancy by the entirety property that goes to Wife, and $2,000 of the checking account, which, we'll assume, Brother can prove he contributed).

	Wife	*Son*
Net Total	$ 256,000	$ 80,000
Applicable Exemptions	− 110,000	− 25,000
Taxable Total	$ 146,000	$ 55,000

	Daughter	Brother
Net Total	$ 35,000	$ 15,000
Applicable Exemptions	– 25,000	– 2,000
Taxable Total	$ 10,000	$ 13,000

Now, each person gets an additional exemption, depending on his or her relation to John. Let's assume that in John's state, spouses get a $100,000 exemption; parents, children, and grandchildren get a $50,000 exemption each; and all other parties get a $5,000 exemption. Obviously, different states will have different exemptions for different relationships. Once you have subtracted the appropriate exemption, you go to the tax tables. Here is the tax schedule for each party:

SURVIVING SPOUSE—FIRST $100,000 FREE.
ON AMOUNTS ABOVE THAT:

A *Taxable Value Equal to or More Than*	B *But Taxable Value Less Than*	C *Tax on Amount in Col. A*	D *Plus Percentage of Tax on Excess over Amount in Col. A*
$ 0	$ 25,000	$ 0	2
25,000	100,000	500	3
100,000	200,000	2,750	5
200,000	—	7,750	7

FATHER, MOTHER, CHILD, OR GRANDCHILD—FIRST
$50,000 FREE. ON AMOUNTS ABOVE THAT:

A *Taxable Value Equal to or More Than*	B *But Taxable Value Less Than*	C *Tax on Amount in Col. A*	D *Plus Percentage of Tax on Excess over Amount in Col. A*
$ 0	$ 25,000	$ 0	3
25,000	75,000	750	5
75,000	150,000	3,250	7
150,000	—	8,500	8

ALL OTHER BENEFICIARIES—FIRST $5,000 FREE.
ON AMOUNTS ABOVE THAT:

A *Taxable Value* *Equal to or* *More Than*	B *But Taxable* *Value Less* *Than*	C *Tax on* *Amount in* *Col. A*	D *Plus Percen-* *tage of Tax on* *Excess over* *Amount in* *Col. A*
$ 0	$ 20,000	$ 0	3
20,000	70,000	600	6
70,000	145,000	3,600	8
145,000	—	9,600	10

Wife's taxable estate was $146,000. You can see from her tax schedule that she would pay $500 + 3 percent of $21,000 = $1,130. Son would pay 3 percent of $5,000, or $150. Daughter would pay nothing, since the $50,000 exemption is in excess of her taxable total of $10,000. Brother would pay 3 percent on $8,000, or $240.

As mentioned earlier, because the amounts payable to the state for inheritance tax are quite small, especially in comparison with the potential federal estate tax, most planning focuses on the reduction of federal estate taxes. One obvious point, however, is that only under very rare circumstances should you make your insurance payable to your estate. If it is payable to your estate, federal estate tax and state inheritance tax (in most states) will apply, and the proceeds will be included in your probate estate, which means that your creditors can get at them and you will have to pay probate fees on them as well. It is always better planning to make your insurance proceeds payable to a named beneficiary (which can even be a life insurance trust that you have set up).

Putting It All Together

AS MUCH AS it would be nice to, it's really impossible to end the book with one example, or one list of "Things to ask yourself about your estate plan," or one crafty bit of advice that will "put it all together" for you. That's because the area of estate planning is too complex to allow for it, and because what might be right for one person may not be right for another. If you've read the book through, you know more than most people ever know about estate planning. You've doubtless thought of questions that this book doesn't answer. That doesn't mean the answers don't exist—they do. It's just that, in the interest of length and cost, only the most "usual" situations and estate plans were discussed.

So is there any way for you to get the answers? Sure. You

should see an expert in the area. From the simplest estate and objectives to the most complex, an expert can help you get your thoughts in order, answer your questions, possibly save your beneficiaries some taxes, and certainly save your family a lot of problems when you pass from the here to the hereafter.

Glossary

Administrator A male person or corporation appointed to probate an Intestate's estate. Administratrix is a female with the same job.

Annual Exclusion The right to exclude from federal gift tax the first $10,000 given in any year by a Donor to a Donee.

Attorney-in-Fact See Power of Attorney.

Beneficiary A person who receives benefits under a Will or from a Trust.

Codicil A supplement that adds to, deletes from, or changes the provisions of a Will.

Contingent Beneficiary A Beneficiary who receives a benefit only if a future event occurs.

Curtesy   The right of a widower to take a share of his deceased wife's estate. Now called Elective Share in many states.

Decedent   A person who is deceased.

Donee   A person who receives a gift.

Donor   A person who makes a gift.

Dower   The right of a widow to take a share of her deceased husband's estate. Now called Elective Share in many states.

Elective Share   The right of a surviving spouse to take one third (or other fraction) of the deceased spouse's net Probate Estate. Sometimes called "forced share."

Estate Tax   The tax on the estate of a deceased person. Usually, the Federal Estate Tax. Compare Inheritance Tax.

Executor   A male person or a corporation appointed to probate the estate of a testate person. Executrix is a female with the same job. This term is commonly used instead of Administrator (-trix) and Personal Representative.

Fiduciary   A person who exercises rights or manages property for a Beneficiary. A Trustee, an Administrator, and an Executor are examples of a Fiduciary.

Guardian of the Person   One who has the legal care and control over a minor or an incompetent adult.

Guardian of the Property   One who has the legal care and control over the property of a minor or incompetent adult.

Heir   A person who takes a share of an Intestate's Intestacy Property.

Inheritance Tax   The tax on recipients of a deceased's property. Often used to include the Federal Estate Tax.

Intestacy Property   The property of an Intestate person

that will be distributed to his or her heirs under the Laws of Intestacy. Intestacy Property generally excludes life insurance, property held by the Intestate person as a Tenant by the Entirety or as a Joint Tenant with Right of Survivorship, and property held in a Living Trust.

Intestate   As an adjective, to be without a valid will; as a noun, one who has no valid will.

Irrevocable   Cannot be revoked, amended, changed, or canceled.

Issue   Offspring or descendants. Your children, grandchildren, great-grandchildren, and so forth, are your Issue.

Joint Tenancy with Right of Survivorship   A way of holding Title to property by two or more persons so that when one person dies his or her share automatically goes to the surviving joint tenants, and not under the deceased's Will or under the Laws of Intestacy.

Laws of Intestacy   The laws of a state that dictate to whom the Intestacy Property of a person dying Intestate will be distributed.

Legacy   A gift of Personal Property made in a will. The same thing as a "bequest."

Letters Testamentary   Issued by the probate court, these authorize the Executor to probate the estate of the deceased.

Life Insurance Trust   A Living Trust into which proceeds from a life insurance policy will flow. It may also hold other property.

Living Trust   A Trust established by a Settlor while he or she is living.

Living Will   A writing that requests that life will not be prolonged by artificial means when death becomes inevitable.

Per Capita A way of dividing a gift so that each designated person gets an equal share.

Per Stirpes A way of dividing a gift so that the children of a deceased person divide only the share their parent would have taken if living.

Personal Property Property that is movable. Any property that is not Real Property.

Personal Representative A term meaning Administrator (-trix) or Executor (-trix). Sometimes used, but term has not yet gained widespread understanding or acceptance.

Pour-Over Will A Will that transfers all, or a portion, of an estate into a preexisting Living Trust.

Power of Attorney A writing by which a person (the "principal") authorizes another person (Attorney-in-Fact) to act for him or her in a limited or general capacity.

Probate The process of settling an estate of a deceased and transferring his property to his Heirs or Beneficiaries. Done under the supervision of the Probate Court.

Probate Estate Property held in the deceased's name alone, or his or her percentage interest in property held as a Tenant in Common, that is being probated.

Real Property Land, and fixed improvements and growing things thereon. Contrast to Personal Property.

Residue The remainder of an estate after specific gifts are made.

Revocable Subject to being revoked, canceled, changed, or modified.

Settlor A person who establishes a Trust.

Sprinkling Trust A Trust under which the Trustee has discretion to make distributions among two or more

Beneficiaries in accordance with a guideline (such as need).

Tenancy by the Entirety   A Joint Tenancy with "right of survivorship" where the only two tenants (owners) are husband and wife.

Tenancy in Common   A way of holding Title to property by two or more persons so that when one persons dies, his or her share is disposed of by a Will or as part of his or her other Intestacy Property.

Testamentary Trust   A Trust established in a Will.

Testator   A male person who makes a valid Will. Testatrix is a female person who makes a valid Will.

Title   Ownership.

Trust   An arrangement whereby one person (the Settlor) transfers Real and/or Personal Property to another person (the Trustee) to hold for the benefit of a third person (the Beneficiary) or the Settlor.

Trustee   The person or institution that holds Trust property, manages it, and distributes it to the Beneficiaries.

Will   A document which, if executed in accordance with legal requirements, will distribute property held in your name alone and your interest in a Tenancy in Common. Usually, it will not govern life insurance, property held as a Joint Tenant with right of survivorship or as a Tenant by the Entirety, or property held in a Living Trust.

About the Author

DAVID C. LARSEN was born in Honolulu, and studied law at the University of California at Los Angeles, where he was editor in chief of the *UCLA-Alaska Law Review*. Since 1975 he has taught wills and probate at the University of Hawaii Law School. He has also taught courses on probate and estate planning to community and professional groups, as well as to other attorneys, through the Hawaii Institute of Continuing Legal Education. Mr. Larsen lives with his wife and infant daughter in Honolulu, where he is an attorney specializing in wills, trusts, and estate planning.